LET ME ILLUSTRATE

AUTHOR OF:

THE GOSPEL OF CHRIST
DEFINITE DECISIONS
PASTOR'S RECORD OF FUNERALS
PASTOR'S RECORD OF WEDDINGS
SERMONS IN OUTLINE
SEED FOR SERMONS
HEART SERMONS IN OUTLINE
THE GOSPEL PREACHER AND HIS PREACHING
EVANGELISTIC SERMONS IN OUTLINE

LET ME ILLUSTRATE

Spiritual Truth
in
Personal Experiences

JEROME O. WILLIAMS

BROADMAN PRESS
NASHVILLE, TENNESSEE

Printed in the United States of America
7.5MH533

To

All Friends Who Seek

a

Vital Experience

with

The Lord Each Day

CONTENTS

see page 13

INTRODUCTION

In November of 1924 many messengers were on the train from Birmingham to Anniston, Alabama, to attend the annual meeting of the Alabama Baptist Convention. I sat down beside Dr. L. L. Gwaltney, editor of the *Alabama Baptist*, and said to him, "Dr. Gwaltney, why don't you publish in the columns of the *Alabama Baptist* each week a rich and uplifting spiritual experience from some of our great leaders like Drs. Crumpton, Davidson, Dickenson, Phillips, or Stakely?"

Dr. Gwaltney replied, in his characteristic way: "Boy, you've got sense; I have written each one of these brethren asking them for an account of personal spiritual experiences of that kind that we might publish in the paper every week, and up to this moment not a one of them has replied." Then he turned to me and said, "I will make you a proposition: If you will write the experiences, I will publish them."

My reply was, "I will do this: I will write a half dozen of the type of experiences that I have in mind and send them to you. You may read them over and evaluate them. If you consider them worthy, print them; and I will send others by the time these are printed. If you do not think they are worthy of publication, throw them in the waste-basket, and nothing else will be said."

I went back home and wrote the six articles, giving the general title of "Events That Illustrate," with a title to each article. Each began with a passage of Scripture and related a brief experience. I sent them to Dr. Gwaltney, and he published the first one in the issue of the *Alabama Baptist* of April 2, 1925, and wrote a letter thanking me for the idea and articles. He stated that he would continue to publish them so long as I would write them. This continued weekly for about seven years, when I became so involved with other matters that I requested release. However, since that time, I have continued to make a record of certain outstanding spiritual experiences and to use them in connection with my work.

These personal experiences of spiritual truth are just a few out of a large number which I have had through the years. They are presented for publication on the request of many, many friends through the years. I trust they will be a blessing to large circles of friends who may read them and that they will be helpful illustrative material for Christian workers such as preachers, teachers, and those who conduct devotional services in prayer meetings, missionary circle meetings, class meetings, and other types of religious services.

If these experiences should prove helpful in lifting other people nearer to the Lord and enriching their lives, the desires of the author will be accomplished.

LET ME ILLUSTRATE

1

Assurance

BRIGHTER AND BRIGHTER

Sometime ago I had the joy of assisting a pastor in a series of revival meetings. One afternoon we were out calling on some of the lost people and others who were not active in the church. As we came near a good home, the pastor said, "Suppose we stop here a moment and have a prayer with a good old grandmother who has been ill and will not be able to attend any of the services."

We went into the house and found the gray-haired grandmother, eighty-four years of age. Her pleasant smile and beautiful face revealed the grace of God beaming from her life. We read a passage of Scripture and had a prayer, asking the blessings of the Lord on this grandmother and the home. Then a word was said by the pastor about how she had suffered. She replied, "Well, I'll have all the pain while I'm here."

"Yes," the pastor replied, "we are told that in the next life 'there shall be no more death, neither sorrow, nor crying, neither shall there be any more pain' " (Rev. 21:4).

Then the good grandmother replied with utmost confidence and radiant joy: "I'm building on that promise. I have been going toward that land now for seventy-one years, for I became a Christian when I was thirteen. I love the way of Christ, and it grows brighter and brighter all the time."

How these words did nerve us for the task of seeking others for *the way!* It is a good way, and leads to eternal life and happiness where Christ and all his redeemed will rejoice evermore in the brightness of the eternal Father.

"But the path of the just is as the shining light, that shineth more and more unto the perfect day" (Prov. 4:18).

"I CAN'T DROP IT NOW"

One Sunday morning years ago, we were just about ready to go to Sunday school. Our precious little four-year-old girl was ready, and she had a dime in her hand for the offering. Like all children, she couldn't be still, and in her activities she dropped the dime. It rolled about in the room and finally landed in a dark corner under some of the furniture. It was soon found, and as she received it in her little hand again, she said, "I'll try to hold on to it now."

Soon we were off, and as we went on to the church she gave to me the precious little hand which held the dime and said, "Daddy, you had better hold my hand." It was a joy for me to fold my hand over hers. Thus we went along for some steps. As my hand was folded firmly over hers, she looked up into my face and said, "I can't drop it now, can I, Daddy?"

So with the believer. There is a way for the believer to be sure of salvation. Believe the Word of Christ, and completely commit all into the hands of Christ. The soul is then in the hand of Christ, enfolded in the firm, strong hand of the Father, and it is impossible for it to perish.

Jesus said, "I give unto them eternal life; and they shall never perish, neither shall any man pluck them out of my hand. My Father, which gave them me, is greater than all; and no man is able to pluck them out of my Father's hand" (John 10:28-29).

The person who surrenders to Christ and trusts him implicitly is "preserved in Jesus Christ" (Jude 1); "hid with Christ in God" (Col. 3:3); and "kept by the power of God" (1 Peter 1:5).

> Blessed assurance, Jesus is mine!
> Oh, what a foretaste of glory divine!
> Heir of salvation, purchase of God,
> Born of His Spirit, washed in His blood.

"JESUS TELLS ME SO"

I had been watching the children in the homes of the people of our church. In one home there was a little girl who had given evidence of saving faith in Christ and had expressed her desire to follow Christ in baptism and into the membership of the church.

When I took her aside for a personal conversation about her faith in Christ, she said to me, "I'm very sure I am a Christian!" I then said to her, "How do you know you are a Christian?" The little girl hesitated for a moment and then made answer positively, "Jesus tells me so in my heart." That was a difficult question to put to a child, but her answer was sublime in its truthfulness and simplicity.

That is the way every person can be sure. "The Spirit itself beareth witness with our spirit, that we are the children of God" (Rom. 8:16). "The word is nigh thee, even in thy mouth, and in thy heart: that is, the word of faith, which we preach; that if thou shalt confess with thy mouth the Lord Jesus, and shalt believe in thine heart that God hath raised him from the dead, thou shalt be saved. For with the heart man believeth unto righteousness" (Rom. 10:8-10).

PERFECT ASSURANCE

A very old woman was in the membership of a church which it was my pleasure to serve as pastor. She had passed her ninety-second birthday. A remarkable thing about her was that during all these years she had been blessed with almost perfect use of her physical senses. She was born on foreign soil and brought to this country when only a child. She found and accepted Christ as personal Saviour early in life. She was married here, and lived a very simple life of faith, love, and hope. Now in her declining days, she was alone, having outlived the other members of her family.

One long, severe winter she had a case of influenza. It was too much for her, and, as spring drew near, she grew weaker. It was soon found that she could not live much longer. The doctor was faithful to her and informed her of her condition.

One morning, as the doctor was leaving the home, I was entering. On inquiry about her condition, the doctor informed me that she could not live long, possibly a day or perhaps a week, and the end would come. I went on in the home, sat down by the bedside of the good old grandmother, and talked at length with her. She was happy and even jovial. She enjoyed talking of days gone by, but her chief interest was in the happy days to come. We quoted some verses of Scripture and sang "What a Friend We Have in Jesus," and prayed together.

Then, after some further conversation, I said to her, "Grandmother, do you know you will not be here much longer?"

She looked into my face with a pleasing smile and an expression of perfect satisfaction beaming from her countenance, and said, "Yes, I know it, and I am just waiting for the time to come for me to go to a better home."

I then remarked to her, "All the way is perfectly clear, isn't it?" And she quoted in her own beautiful way the words of the apostle Paul (2 Tim. 1:12): "I know whom I have believed, and am thoroughly convinced that he is able to keep that which I have committed unto him against that day."

That afternoon, about six o'clock, the Master came into this home and called for Grandmother. She went to peaceful sleep here, to awake in the land of perfect peace, joy, and happiness.

The religion of the Lord Jesus Christ had more meaning to me after that morning, and it has been a great joy for me to witness for him and his power to save and satisfy the human soul. The glory of the Christian religion is found in that it satisfies the longing of the human heart. Deep in the heart of every human being is a desire to worship, a longing for God. This is true with the people of every nation, every tongue, and every tribe the world over. Christ can meet and satisfy this longing.

2

Bible

A TINY BIBLE

I shall never forget the first meeting of a Baptist association that I attended, just four miles from our home. Cotton had opened early that season, and we had worked steadily to gather it. Things went well, the cotton was gathered and sold, the new suit was bought, and a new hat, collar, and tie came along with it. Joy reigned when we were in the two-horse wagon and on our way to the association. It was a day of first things with me—first long trousers, first real hat, first white collar, first red tie—all dressed up and on the way to my first Baptist association.

It was a great day, and I heard some of the leading preachers speak. Dr. Frank Willis Barnett was there representing the *Alabama Baptist*, which he owned and edited at that time. When the "dinner-on-the-ground" was over, Dr. Barnett yelled to everybody that he was going to speak in the church immediately. The people filled the building. When he began, he showed a tiny Bible about the size of a man's thumb. To prove that it was a real Bible, he threw it out into the congregation, and it fell on my head and into my hands. I looked at it, loved it, and how I did want to keep it! This, along with all other references to the Bible in this meeting, increased my love for it, my faith in it, and my devotion to it.

"The law of the Lord is perfect, converting the soul: the testimony of the Lord is sure, making wise the simple. The statutes of the Lord are right, rejoicing the heart: the commandment of the Lord is pure, enlightening the eyes. The fear of the Lord is clean, enduring for ever: the judgments of the Lord are true and righteous altogether. More to be desired are they than gold, yea, than much fine gold: sweeter also than honey and the honeycomb" (Psalm 19: 7-10).

"HE BEGAN TO READ"

At one church where I conducted a brief revival meeting, at the morning hour of worship every day was a good man who worked at night as a clerk in a large hotel. He was a Catholic. A copy of the New Testament was given to him, and during the quiet hours of the early morning while all others were sleeping, he began to read it. It was appealing to him, and he greatly enjoyed it. He read it through several times and became a true believer in the Lord Jesus Christ.

The man made a profession of faith in Christ as his personal Saviour, united with the church as a candidate for baptism, and after that was received into the fellowship of the church. He has been a faithful, loyal, and true member of that church ever since, although he had some difficulty in doing so, for his wife and other members of his family belong yet to the other faith. But he is true and follows Christ to the best of the light that has been given him.

There is power in the Word of God. There is power in

the gospel of Jesus Christ. It is the power of God unto salvation to all who will believe. Our great need is that the gospel of Christ may have a chance in the hearts of people of this busy age.

"For I am not ashamed of the gospel of Christ: for it is the power of God unto salvation to every one that believeth; to the Jew first, and also to the Greek" (Rom. 1:6).

"SOMETHING TO TELL YOU"

"For the word of God is quick, and powerful, and sharper than any twoedged sword, piercing even to the dividing asunder of soul and spirit, and of the joints and marrow, and is a discerner of the thoughts and intents of the heart" (Heb. 4:12).

Yes, the Word is quick, powerful, pointed, and piercing. It is the sword of the Spirit. It is the thought of God. It is man's weapon of war against the sin of the world.

A young woman, a very beautiful Christian character, came to me after chapel service in one of our Baptist schools and said, "I have something to tell you." She then told me her name and the place of her home, and inquired if I remembered conducting a series of revival services in a church near by some years ago. I assured her that I did remember the place and the meeting.

She then told me that she attended the meeting as an unconverted person. She reminded me that I had requested the congregation to repeat again and again the passage of Scripture, "God is our refuge and strength, a very present help in trouble" (Psalm 46:1). This verse of Scripture went to her heart, and she was soon troubled about her soul. She was convicted of sin. She felt the need of a Saviour. In her trouble she called on the Lord, and he heard her cry and saved her soul.

Later, the Lord called her for special service, and soon she will go out to use his Word in leading many others to him.

His Word is powerful. The gospel of Christ is the power of God unto salvation to all who will believe.

THE BIBLE IN HIS HANDS

It was the morning of November 7, 1918. The place was in the heart of the Battle of the Argonne in France during World War I. Our American soldiers had made an advance on the enemy over an open field on a hill, and in the effort many of them had received fatal wounds. We went forward to find and to help the wounded.

Later in the morning I came to the body of one of our brave men in the edge of the woods, cold in death. His body had been peppered with bullets from a machine gun. After receiving the fatal wounds, he fell to the ground, drew his coat about his body, took his Bible from his haversack, placed the haversack under his head, and rested the Bible in his open left hand on his chest. The Book was open at the fourteenth chapter of the Gospel of John. When I found him, his index finger pointed to the sixth verse of that great chapter.

I lifted the cold hand, took the blessed Book out of the other, turned to the flyleaf and saw that the Book was lovingly presented to him by his mother. At the bottom of the flyleaf he had written in his own hand, "The following passages constitute the motto for my life," and he had listed three references and signed his name.

The first reference was John 14:6: "Jesus said unto him, I am the way, the truth, and the life: no man cometh unto the Father, but by me." In this passage, the cold, dead finger of my comrade pointed to the Lord Jesus Christ as the only hope for a sinful soul and the only Saviour for the lost world. There is no other way to be saved from sin. Reject him, and all is ruin, loss, and failure.

The second Scripture reference in the soldier's devotion was Matthew 6:33: "Seek ye first the kingdom of God, and his righteousness; and all these things shall be added unto you." When the soul finds eternal life through faith in Christ, it then has the joyous privilege of working with God in the proclamation of the gospel and the extension of the kingdom on earth. Blessed is the life that will put his kingdom first, even before physical necessities of life, or pleasure, or power, or popularity, or any other objective. The lad's life pointed to the greatest service of saved people.

The third reference in the soldier's motto was Romans 8:28: "We know that all things work together for good to them that love God, to them who are the called according to his purpose." How could he say it? How could he believe it? How could he live by it? How could he die with it? Yes, the loving hand of Providence will see to it that all things in life will work together for good for those who will love God devotedly. Human eyes may not see it, but the all-seeing eye of God sees, and he knows and declares it. It is good to love and trust God. It is good to trust all to him. It is good to learn the will of God and to let him have his way.

Thus, the cold, dead finger of my comrade pointed to the four most vital and fundamental things of life: Jesus Christ, the only Saviour from sin; the church and kingdom, the place for the most important service of life; the Holy Bible, the sufficient rule and guide for our faith and practice; and the providence of God, the only place of safety and security for our soul.

I fell to my knees by the dead body of my comrade that morning and prayed earnestly, "Lord, let me live, and I'll be true to thee, to Christ, to the Bible, and to the kingdom." The Lord answered my prayer and allowed me to live. Now I go up and down our land, calling my fellow Baptists to loyalty to the church, the Bible, the Christ, and the living God.

THE LITTLE RED TESTAMENT

When our large family lived in the country, Father was anxious for the children to know something about the Bible and to become true Christians and effective servants of the Lord.

At the fireside one evening, Father promised to purchase, the next time he went to town, a New Testament for each of the older children of the family. Naturally I felt bad because that left me out. My position in the family was between the old and the young—young enough to wear the old clothes of the older boys, and old enough to have to take care of the younger children. But before time to make the trip to town, I made it a point to get on the good side of Father and request him to include my name on the list and get a New Testament for me. He asked me if

I could read it. Immediately I got the family Bible, placed it in a chair before him, and the Book fell open at the fourteenth chapter of the Gospel of John. I knew that by memory, so I proceeded to read for him. When the going was difficult, I closed the Book and put it away. He made no promise to get the Testament for me.

The time came for the weekly trip to town. Late in the afternoon, when Father returned, he gave my eldest brother a package wrapped in brown paper and tied with a white cotton string, which looked to me large enough to contain four copies of the New Testament. We children were thrilled as we followed our brother into the house and gathered about the table on which he placed the package. Brother removed the wrapping from the package and arranged on the table four of the most beautiful books I have ever seen. One had a black binding, another brown, another blue, and another red. Brother then said to the anxious group, "We will allow the youngest of the four to take his choice." Up to that time I had not been noticed. Now, I became very important. There was not a moment of hesitation. You can see me now reaching for that New Testament with a red binding. My soul thrilled within me. I became somebody immediately.

It is my firm conviction that each child in every home should have a copy of the New Testament as early in life as he is able to read. It should be his own individual book, and he should be encouraged to read it and be instructed in its teachings.

"Search the scriptures; for in them ye think ye have eternal life: and they are they which testify of me" (John 5:39). "Then opened he their understanding, that they might understand the scriptures" (Luke 24:45).

3

Christian

Our telephone rang, and when I answered, the troubled and trembling voice of a young mother in the church membership requested me to come to her home immediately. As I went on the way, I remembered that there were three people in the home, the father, the mother, and the young child. The father was not a Christian. He defied God and denied his Word and had nothing to do with the church. The mother was a most devout Christian and faithful member of the church. The child was less than a year old.

When I reached the home, the mother was walking up and down the hallway, wringing her hands. When I inquired the trouble, she pointed to a room to one side. In the room were the father, a nurse, some friends, one of the best doctors in the city, all gathered about the bed of the child, who was sick unto death. When I asked the doctor about the condition of the child, he replied: "There is no hope. She will be gone in a few minutes. I am waiting now to sign a death certificate."

Since I could be of no service at the bedside, I went to the young mother and invited her to be seated in the rear of the hallway. When we were seated, I said to her: "Now, Mary, it looks to me like you had just as well get ready for the end in this matter. For the sake of Christ, and as an example to Charles, your husband, I want to ask you to be brave and courageous in this sorrow. You have the Lord to help you, and with his help you can bear all sorrow. Charles does not have this help. For his sake you can be brave." After we had prayed for a moment, the door opened, and the nurse came quietly down the hallway. She placed her hand on the shoulder of the mother and said, "Mary, Pauline is gone." The young mother lifted her hands heavenward and cried, "Oh my Lord, what shall I do? My only child is gone!" She was assured that there was nothing to do except to trust all to the Lord.

The next day we came for the final service. The reading of some verses of Scripture assured all of the love of Jesus for little children. After we sang some songs and sought the blessings of the Lord in prayer, friends looked again on the little face. The father and mother came toward the casket, hand in hand, and heart in heart. When they were near the casket, the husband released the hand of his wife and turned to go out of the room, wailing in most bitter terms, "Good-by, Pauline! Good-by! I'll never see you again!" The mother went to the casket, looked into the little face, caressed the cold, small hands, kissed the lifeless cheeks, and then said to the little one: "Good-by, Pauline! But not good-by forever. I'll see you again in the morning of the resurrection."

All who looked upon that scene and lived through those experiences went away assured again and again that there is eternal comfort in the presence and power of Jesus in the hour of sorrow. Christ can comfort sorrowing souls.

Jesus said, "Let not your heart be troubled: ye believe in God, believe also in me" (John 14:1).

"Come unto me, all ye that labour and are heavy laden, and I will give you rest" (Matt. 11:28).

JUST SPINNING AROUND

While conducting a revival meeting in one of our churches, I went home with a young couple for the noon meal. Though I had known the young people many years and they had been married for more than a year, this was my first time to visit in their home.

As we entered the home, so pleasant and beautiful, we heard a whining, pleading cry coming from some place. Not being able to know the source or to recognize the maker of the noise, and being just a bit puzzled, I said, "What? Is that a child about here?" The young people looked at each other and smiled, and then laughed aloud as they replied: "No, there is no child here. That is our poodle in his box on the back porch."

We then went to the back porch and saw the poor little fellow in a tiny box, with heavy weights on the lid. He looked anxiously to his master and begged earnestly to be released. Soon the master removed the heavy weights, lifted the lid from the box and freed the little dog. How he did rejoice! He leaped on the box, on the floor, on the ground, up to his master, and was just spinning around, leaping, and rejoicing. His whole being was thrilled with joy that the master had released him.

How like the burdened soul! The word "joy" in our language is from a root word *giel*, meaning "to spin around." That is just what the poodle did when he was

released. Before conversion the soul feels the heavy burden
of sin. Sorrow comes with conviction. Christ comes, and
is accepted by faith; he lifts the burden of sin, turns grief
into joy and darkness into light, and the soul is thrilled
with the unspeakable joy. He makes the heart happy; he
makes the life glad. This joy should be with the believer
through this life on earth and should greatly increase in
the life to come.

"That they might have joy fulfilled in themselves" (John
17:13). "Ask, and ye shall receive, that your joy may be
full" (John 16:24.) "And your heart shall rejoice, and
your joy no man taketh from you" (John 16:22). Believ-
ing, ye rejoice with joy unspeakable and full of glory"
(1 Peter 1:8).

POWER TO MAKE A BAD MAN GOOD

Some years ago I was studying the divinity of Christ.
In prayer, the thought came to me that Christ is the Son
of God because he has power to make a bad man good.
That very thing had been done in the community where
I was.

A man in that community had been a bad character. He
spent his time gambling, his money for drink, and lived
a shameful life, while his poor wife and five children
suffered for food and clothing and comforts in a hovel in
a back alley. One Sunday afternoon the man attended a
special service for men and boys. The message of the
Lord and the Spirit of the Lord convicted the man of sin.
He was saved, and joined the church.

After the man was converted, he went to work, saved his money, moved his family into a nice house on a good street, and provided food, clothing, books, and many luxuries for them. He became a regular attendant on the services of the church, was prosperous, and the family was happy.

In order to discover the truth of my conviction, I decided to visit this home to talk with the wife of this man. When I arrived, however, I found that he was slightly ill and had not gone to work. I sat in front of the little fire in the living room of the home, with the husband to my left and the wife to my right. After passing the greetings of the morning, I said to the wife, "Mrs. B., I want you to help me write a sermon." She replied: "I cannot do that; I do not know how to write a sermon. If it were to feed the hungry, make clothes for orphans, make a visit, or clean the church, I could do that, but I cannot write a sermon."

Then I said to her, "I am trying to write a sermon, and it will help me greatly if you will tell me whether you think Christ has power to make a bad man good."

With this she arose and passed around my chair to her husband and said to him, "John, you should be able to tell the man that." He arose and took her hand in his, and, passing his finger over an ugly scar on her arm, said to her, "Dear, do you remember the morning I put that there?" She replied, "Yes, John, but I have forgiven you, and it is all right." He then drew her collar down and looked at the scar he had placed on the back of her neck and said, "You remember the morning I came in after a night of gambling and drinking and struck you there, and the doctor came and took six stitches to heal the wound?" She replied, "Yes, I remember it, but I have forgiven you." He kissed the scar and looked into the face of his wife and said: "Dear, I will never do that again. I am a different man now."

The husband then came over to me, shook hands, and said, "Preacher, you can go and tell the world that Christ has power to make a bad man good." I said: "Praise the Lord! That is what I wanted. Thank you."

Christ is the Son of God. "Thou art the Christ, the Son of the living God" (Matt. 16:16). It is true that "the blood of Jesus Christ his Son cleanseth us from all sin" (1 John 1:7), and "If any man be in Christ, he is a new creature" (2 Cor. 5:17).

THE ELDER BROTHER

There were nine boys and three girls in our family. When we were children on the farm in Chilton County, Alabama, our school days and advantages were somewhat limited. All luxuries of life were also limited, for we lived on a rented farm until the oldest child was almost grown. Being poor is no dishonor, and one of the glories of American life is that children from the most humble homes may rise to even the highest stations among us.

We walked three miles to attend the Cross Road School a few weeks during the winter and a few days in the summer. The school was not much more than a great gathering of children without a purpose, for there were about eighty children in seven grades, all in one room, with only one teacher. But it was the best we had, and we made the best of it.

When school was out, the children went east, west, north,

and south. From our home there was usually a small army, among whom were two of my older and larger brothers. We mingled with the crowd on our road. Upon these older boys rested much responsibility, for they were charged with the care and keeping of the younger ones along the way.

In a crowd like this, all going the same way at the same time, it was easy for the boys to stir up a few fights. I do not suppose I was any exception to the rule, and so I had my share of the difficulties. Occasionally I would come to a clash with a boy whose fighting ability was superior to mine. In such instances I would make for one of my larger brothers and stand erect by his side. Then, with fist ready to fight, and with a look of great bravery and determination in my eyes, I would say, "Now come on, and we'll settle it!" The elder brother was always ready to help, and it brought great comfort.

From that small country school I passed on through the other schools, and then out into the great school of life. I have always encountered difficulties along the way, which have often been far more grave than those of early days in school. In this big battle of life in the world, I have always found great comfort and help in the Elder Brother, who is a "friend that sticketh closer than a brother." When trials, troubles, difficulties, disappointments, and disagreements come, I find him ever near my side to take my part.

The great apostle Paul said, "I can do all things through Christ which strengtheneth me" (Phil. 4:13). "The Spirit itself beareth witness with our spirit, that we are the children of God: and if children, then heirs; heirs of God, and joint-heirs with Christ; if so be that we suffer with him, that we may be also glorified together" (Rom. 8:16-17).

THE SOURCE OF LIGHT

It was years ago that we were visiting in a big old country home in Texas. One evening, while we were eating dinner, the light began to grow dim. The father in the home knew at once the trouble—the light was made by acetylene gas, and the supply was giving out. On inquiry, it was found that the supply of ingredients at the home was exhausted, and a messenger was sent posthaste to borrow the need from a neighbor. Soon the lights were shining again.

There is a source of light for our spiritual lives that never wanes; the supply is never exhausted. It is fresh every morning, free at noontime, and abundant in the evening. Christ is the source of the spiritual light. He can never be exhausted. When he was here on earth, he said, "I am the light of the world: he that followeth me shall not walk in the darkness, but shall have the light of life" (John 8:12).

Christ is the true light of the world that lighteth every man. When he had taught some of his disciples, he said to them, "Ye are the light of the world" (Matt. 5:14). He is the source of our light, and when we are in intimate touch with him, we may reflect his light to men.

"Let your light so shine before men, that they may see your good works, and glorify your Father which is in heaven" (Matt. 5:16).

THE TRUE LIGHT

Some weeks ago, in making a trip by train, it was necessary for me to change cars at a small town very early in the morning. The change necessitated a wait of about two hours. When we got off the train, it was very dark; yet I had been on the train all night, and had another day before me; so I decided to take a walk in the bracing atmosphere of the dark morning.

A five-minute walk took me to the heart of town. There I saw every effort of man to cope with darkness. The street lights were hanging at every corner; the White Way was found on the main street; the show windows were all lighted; yet how feeble were the lights to cope with darkness in the world about.

Then I walked to an elevated place and looked again at the dense darkness covering the earth and the feeble efforts to drive it away. After waiting for a time, the sun began to show light in the east, and soon, in a gloriously clear morning, the sun was brightly lighting every nook and corner. What a change when the sun came!

John was a "burning and shining light," but he came only to announce the coming of the great Light, the true Light, the Christ, which lighteth every man that cometh into the world. When Jesus came, he said, "As long as I am in the world, I am the light of the world" (John 9:5). When Jesus had taught his disciples, he said, "Ye are the light of the world" (Matt. 5:14). "Then spake Jesus again unto them, saying, I am the light of the world: he that followeth me shall not walk in darkness, but shall have the light of life" (John 8:12).

Only in Christ can we cope with the darkness of this world.

TO EVERY CREATURE

It was my privilege while in Europe during World War I to try to preach the gospel to the people of eight nationalities in one day. During the day, a message was delivered to some of our American soldiers, to English soldiers, to some French people through an interpreter, to German prisoners through an interpreter, and so on through the day. Late in the afternoon I tried to preach to five hundred Chinese laborers who had done a day's work, and after the evening meal, had gathered in a large Y.M.C.A building. To make this most difficult, I had to preach through two interpreters, one who understood English and French, and the other, French and Chinese.

Try to get the attention of the men, I said to them, "Is there anyone here from near Canton, China?" When this question was understood, five hands went up. I then said, "I have a brother in Canton." This aroused interest, and the men opened their eyes and mouths. Back in the crowd, one of the men uttered a strange sentence, and when it came to me, it was this: "The man wants to know what your brother is doing in Canton."

There was my chance! For an hour, I stood there seeking to let the men know that my brother was in China telling the people that Christ is the only person in all the world who can save a soul from sin. The effort was most difficult, because the men did not seem to understand what I meant by "grace and mercy," "repentance and belief," and "trust and obey."

I went to my cot that night completely exhausted, and, on my knees, said, "Lord, this task of making Christ known to all the people of all the nations of all the earth is a supreme task." It is the great task of the church. It is the greatest task required at the hands of believers.

This is no child's play. It is no woman's club affair. It is not a luncheon club affair. It requires men with blood in their veins, iron in their blood, the grace of God in their hearts, and determination in their souls. It requires men like John Knox of old, who prayed, "Lord, give me Scotland, or I die."

Jesus said to his disciples, "Go ye into all the world, and preach the gospel to every creature" (Mark 16:15).

WHAT CHRIST GIVES

One of our missionaries told me of a visit he made to a mission station in Korea some years ago. A congregation of believers had gathered to hear him speak. He asked the question, "What has Christ given to you?" Immediately the people began to speak out of the fulness of their hearts and out of experiences with Christ. "Forgiveness," cried one. "Joy," exclaimed another. "Strength to meet temptations," said a third. "Peace in my soul," asserted another. "Guidance for my life," stated another. A young person arose and cried aloud, "Eternal life!" Then a person who had experienced great sorrow said, "Comfort in sorrow." And thus, one after another, the foreign people witnessed to the matchless gifts of the Christ.

"But my God shall supply all your need according to his riches in glory by Christ Jesus" (Phil. 4:19). "I will give unto him that is athirst of the fountain of the water of life freely" (Rev. 21:6).

4

Conversion

FROM DARKNESS TO LIGHT

It is always a very personal thing for one to tell of his own conversion, but since the days of Paul it has been a way of powerful testimony to the saving grace of Christ. It is a power now, and thus I am glad to relate the story of my conversion.

It occurred when I was a country lad about nine years of age. Mulberry church, in Chilton County, Alabama, was our home church. It was about four miles from our home, and that was a long distance to travel in a two-horse wagon, for two services a day, to attend the revival meeting which was being conducted at the church.

Under the power of the gospel, at a morning service, a pungent conviction of sin came upon me. I felt conscious of guilt. The remorse of a sinner was upon me. I learned that the righteousness of God demanded punishment. Knowing that I deserved the punishment due a sinner was a very heavy burden on my heart, and I left the church feeling a great need of the Saviour.

During the afternoon I left the members of the family and went alone to the back porch, and began to read my little red-bound New Testament to see if I could find the way of life. Soon my brother, who later went to China as a missionary, came to me and asked if I did not think it was time for me to seek Christ as my personal Saviour.

It did not take me long to tell him that I was trying to do that.

My brother then took the Testament and read some of the passages which show the love of God for a sinner, like John 3:16, Romans 5:8, and others. He also read John 3:36, Romans 10:10, and Romans 10:13, and then requested me to call on the name of the Lord, confessing my sin and trusting Christ. He told me how Christ desired to save me, asked me to believe on Christ, accept him as my personal Saviour, and confess him before men. Then he went away and left me alone.

With the burden of sin upon me, and the way clear before me, I went to the grove, not to talk with friends or relatives about the burden of my soul, but to speak earnestly with the Lord, who alone could be the hope of my salvation. Christ assured me again and again that I had only to trust the welfare of my soul to his care. The season of prayer made the way brighter and my soul more hopeful, but the matter was not yet settled.

Soon we were on our way to the church for the evening service. No soul was ever more serious than mine on that journey. When we arrived at the church, the Spirit of the Lord was there. He could be seen in the faces of the people. He could be felt by every heart present. The music was glorious; the prayers were earnest and fervent; the sermon was powerful. My soul was burdened, and my heart was praying Christ to give me the assurance of salvation at that very service.

Soon the sermon was finished, and an opportunity to accept Christ and make a public profession of faith in him was given. The congregation stood, singing "Just As I Am," and I said, "This is the hope of my soul," and a thrill of joy came to me as the all burden was taken away. The angels sang their glorious song of redemption.

When the joy of forgiveness was in my soul, my duty was clear. I immediately walked down the aisle of that old church, gave my hand to the minister, my heart to God, and my life to the church for service.

"This is a faithful saying, and worthy of all acceptation, that Christ Jesus came into the world to save sinners" (1 Tim. 1:15).

"HELP ME GET HIM OVER"

The usual congregation gathered in our church for the Sunday morning worship service. The message was delivered, the invitation was given to all who would accept Christ and unite with the church, and the congregation stood to sing the invitation hymn.

A small boy came forward, confessing his faith in Christ as personal Saviour and desiring to unite with the church as a candidate for baptism. His face was bright and cheerful as he took this important step.

I had talked with the boy during the week, and knew that he was converted and understood just what he was doing. But another word was spoken to him to make sure. Every question was answered with positive assurance.

Some of the staid old deacons of the church thought the boy was too young to know what he was doing. So when his name was placed before the church, there was a long silence. Finally, one of the deacons made a motion rather reluctantly that the boy be received as a candidate for baptism; but the vote of reception was not hearty.

Late that afternoon, when I was in the study making preparation for the evening message, there was a knock at the door. I said, "Come in!" But no one came in; and there was another knock. I arose and opened the door to find William, who had joined the church at the morning hour, standing there with a troubled look on his face.

"Come in, William. You look troubled. Do you think you made a mistake this morning in joining the church?" I said to him.

"No, sir," was the immediate reply. "I never did anything in my life that made me happier. I have Fred down here, and he is not a Christian, and I have been trying all the afternoon to lead him to Christ. I cannot make it, and I want you to help me get him over."

We went to the outer door to find Fred, the lost boy, who was by this time very anxious about his soul. We returned to the study, and when we were seated, I said, "Now, William, tell me just what you have done so that we may find the trouble and know how to begin."

William began: "When I went home from church today, Mother did not have dinner ready. So I got my Testament and left to find Fred before he got away. All the afternoon we have been out yonder in the woods reading my Testament and praying, but I can't make it clear to him. So I have brought him here, and I want you to help me get him over."

A few other passages of Scripture were read and explained, and the willingness of Christ to save was made plain to the boy. We then carried the matter to the Lord. When I had prayed, William prayed anxiously, and then Fred was requested to tell the Lord how he felt and that he wanted to be saved. In only a few precious moments the light came clearly to the boy and he made a bold confession of faith in Christ.

It was then time for us to go to the Training Union, and we went for this service. Then the evening worship hour came. The congregation was large; the spirit of fellowship was fine; the singing was an inspiration. After a simple but forceful message explaining the way of salvation, the congregation stood to sing the invitation hymn.

At the first word of the hymn, Fred walked down the aisle of the church, gave me his hand, the Lord his heart, and the church his life. He took a bold stand for Christ and the church.

Soon William, who had joined the church at the morning hour, and had worked all the afternoon to lead Fred to Christ, could stand it no longer, and he came down the aisle and stood by Fred and put his arm about him. Some of the deacons looked over at him as if to say, "Yes, I did not think he knew what he was doing this morning."

When the hymn had been completed and the congregation seated, I said, "Fred has come to join our church tonight on profession of his faith in Christ and as a candidate for baptism. I am going to ask William to stand and tell you of their experiences this afternoon."

The young convert, with zeal for the lost and joy that he had won his playmate for Christ, stood like a man and related in clear tones the experiences of the afternoon. He told of his leaving home without dinner, the afternoon in the woods, the visit to the study, the final prayer, and the conversion of Fred. He then made a request that he be baptized at the same time as Fred.

As the boy related this wonderful story, some of the

older people of the church who had never in all their long life led one single soul to the Lord, sat there and wept. There was not a dry eye in the congregation.

When the Lord saves a person, he puts in that heart a desire to see others saved. This truth is illustrated by the life of Isaiah when he was sure his sin was purged and his iniquity taken away. He said to the Lord, "Here am I; send me."

Andrew came from the blessed company of the Master and went for his brother, Simon, saying, "We have found the Messias" (John 1:41).

Paul said, when Jesus had saved him, "Lord, what wilt thou have me to do?" (Acts 9:6).

There are two things that may be done with this desire. It may be cultivated and become a consuming passion of the life, or it may be crushed and finally become almost dead, as was true in the case of the deacons, for not one of them had brought a lost man to me during the two years of service there that I might assist them in leading him to Christ. All should do the former: cultivate a love for lost souls and ability to lead them to Christ.

"He which converteth the sinner from the error of his way shall save a soul from death" (James 5:20).

"HE'S EVERYBODY'S SAVIOUR"

It was during my college days. I was pastor of a village church in central Alabama. Near this village were two large country churches that were good enough to call me to preach for them one Sunday in each month. The summers were spent in the village, from which I could easily reach all engagements.

One Saturday afternoon I was driving out into the country to fill an appointment on Sunday. A heavy rain had just fallen, and the road was very wet and muddy. But, in spite of this, there were many interesting things to see along the way—the most interesting of all being the people.

Before I had gone very far, I overtook a small colored boy about twelve years of age. He was wet all over. His torn, floppy hat was on one side of his head, his ragged shirt unbuttoned, with sleeves rolled above his elbows, his overalls rolled above his knees, and his bare feet covered with mud. He carried a filled bucket in his hand.

As the boy stood to one side of the road, I drove up to him and invited him to ride with me. He made excuses that his feet were too muddy, his clothes too wet, and his skin too black. He did not care to soil the inside of the nice buggy. But after much insistence on my part, he agreed to ride with me, and eased up into the end of the seat, holding his muddy feet and the filled bucket on the outside.

It was soon revealed that the boy was very intelligent. We talked about the community, the homes, the people, both white and colored, the schools for the white and black, and the churches for each. He was familiar with the entire community and talked gladly about all.

The most interesting subject of all to the boy was his own church. He told me gladly about going to Sunday school to learn the Bible and to church to hear the minister preach. He talked freely about his minister and the leaders of his church.

At the right time I said to him, "Jim, do you know

anything about Jesus?" Immediately his face was aglow, and his eyes sparkled as he said, "He's de Saviour."

After asking him if he thought the Lord would save the people of Europe, Asia, and other continents, and getting a positive answer, I said, "Jim, do you believe Jesus will save the colored people?"

He replied, "I tells ye, Boss, he's everybody's Saviour."

I looked into his face and said, "Jim, is he your Saviour?" With this question his head dropped, his eyes flashed far more slowly as great tears began to trickle down his black cheeks.

When he seemed to be ready for further conversation, I said, "Well, Jim, you must have found something wrong with him if you cannot accept him as your personal Saviour."

He was immediate and very positive in his reply that there is nothing wrong at all with Jesus as the Saviour, and said again, "He's everybody's Saviour."

"Well, then," I inquired, "why have you never taken him as your own Saviour?"

He was pathetic as he looked into my face with a most pitiful appeal in his eyes and said, "No one has ever asked me to take him."

After some words of explanation of how Jesus loves and how he is able, ready, willing, and waiting to save, I said to him, "Jim, I am asking you to accept Jesus as your own Saviour here and now."

He lifted his face, and I could see it growing brighter and brighter all the time, and he began to rejoice, saying: "I can accept him! I will accept him! I do accept him! He's my Saviour! I take him as mine!"

All this long drive, and I still did not know what was in that bucket! But when he began to rejoice, he forgot his muddy feet, his wet clothes, and the filled bucket, and spilled buttermilk all over the buggy. He was happy; he rejoiced greatly. He had a reason to rejoice.

As we drove along for a short distance, he came to himself, looked about, and said, "Law, white man, I oughtta got out o' dis buggy two miles back over yonder."

We stopped, and after some minutes he stepped out between the wheels of the buggy and stood there for some minutes trying to tell me how happy he was to have had this ride with me, how glad he was to know Jesus as Saviour, and how he expected to live all his life for Christ and the church.

I advised him to join the church, be baptized, and to be faithful in the work of the church all the time. I offered him my hand and assured him that I would ever be ready and willing to help him in every possible way.

The journey was made to the good country home not so far along, and an inquiry was made about the Negro family. The boy's father owned his farm, was most honorable in all things, and every Sunday went with the children to the church, where he was a deacon.

Some white people may laugh at this event, but let him who laughs do as well as this boy, or even his father.

"All we like sheep have gone astray; we have turned every one to his own way; and the Lord hath laid on him the iniquity of us all" (Isa. 53:6).

"And if any man sin, we have an advocate with the Father, Jesus Christ the righteous: and he is the propitiation for our sins: and not for ours only, but also for the sins of the whole world" (1 John 2:1-2).

THE MOTHER WON

Some years ago there was a fine girl in our congregation who was expecting to graduate from high school. The girl was not a Christian. We were much concerned for her, and she had been the object of much earnest prayer. During a revival meeting at the church in April of that year, the girl requested permission to leave school to attend the morning service. We prayed that she might be convicted of her need of the Saviour that morning. When she went away from the church, it was clear that the Holy Spirit had done his work of conviction.

While we were at the noon meal, the mother of this girl called and requested me to come immediately and talk to the daughter about the Lord. I asked the mother to do certain things until I could get there. She took the daughter alone and read the Bible to her, prayed with her, told her how the Lord Jesus Christ could save her soul, and would save her if she would only believe and trust him.

About that time, I was approaching the home, and the mother ran to meet me and cried, "Oh, Brother Williams, you are too late now!" My reply was, "No, I am not too late; I have come to rejoice with you." Immediately the girl came rushing to her mother and threw her arms about her and said, "Brother Williams, I have the dearest mother in the world. She has always loved me and cared for me, and now she has led me to Christ, and I am a Christian."

I would have felt like a robber if I had stolen the star that rightly belonged to the crown of that mother. "He that winneth souls is wise" (Prov. 11:30).

"And they that be wise shall shine as the brightness of the firmament; and they that turn many to righteousness as the stars for ever and ever" (Dan. 12:3).

5

Devotion

A GOOD MAN

We boys had gone back home for a brief visit. While there we engaged in many conversations about days gone by. We could not but miss some members of the family who had gone on to the richer and fuller life.

One morning we arranged to visit the cemetery near the little country church. In this is the final resting place of the earthly remains of our father. The soil is sacred to each of us. As we approach the silent and sacred place, all hats were off, and we stood there in the summer's sun with bare heads. After standing for sometime in silence, one of the boys, with a slight tremble in his voice and tears in his eyes, turned away, saying, "There is a good man buried there." He was a good man, and every one of his boys would like to be like him.

God be praised for a man who can live such a good life here on earth that when he is in his grave, young men will stand about saying, "Let a double portion of his spirit rest upon me," as was the case when Elijah was taken from Elisha.

The words spoken about Barnabas could have been said of Father. "He was a good man, and full of the Holy Ghost and of faith" (Acts 11:24).

Not all men can become great teachers, preachers, writers, singers, or leaders, but it is within the reach of each one to live a godly life. "Blessed is the man that walketh not in the counsel of the ungodly, nor standeth in the way of sinners, nor sitteth in the seat of the scornful. But his delight is in the law of the Lord" (Psalm 1:1-2).

"ARE YOU THE JESUS MAN?"

The picture of Rev. W. T. Rankin, a Christian minister, can be found on the front page of the *Courier-Journal*, of Louisville, Kentucky, the issue of Tuesday morning, December 3, 1929. The paper gives an account of the minister's falling dead the day before while he was speaking to the Louisville Ministers' Conference in the Warren Memorial Presbyterian Church. It was my lot to be present when it happened.

The good man had just related an event that took place during his ministry as a missionary in the mountains of east Kentucky. He told how he went into a village inhabited by foreigners. The main street of the village was a valley, with small houses on both sides. As he entered the street, children came out of the houses and followed him. He led in singing songs as they walked. Others joined them along the way. When the crowd was near the end of the street, a pleasant-faced man stepped out of one of the houses and came to him and said, "Are you the Jesus man?"

The minister admitted that the question puzzled him at first. He went on to comment, "I could have told him that I am an ordained minister, but he did not ask me that. I could have told him that I am a missionary of Christ, but he did not ask me that. I could have told him that I teach and preach about Jesus, but he did not ask me that. The man asked me the definite question, 'Are you the Jesus man?'"

The minister hesitated a moment, then looked into the faces of his fellow ministers and said earnestly: "Brethren, I am the Jesus man. I seek to live daily the spirit of Jesus. When he comes, I shall be ready to go home with him and live with him forever." With these last words, he began to wane, fell to the floor, and was gone in one minute.

It is the highest ideal for Christians to seek to live like Jesus, worthy of him and his gospel to a lost world. "I beseech you therefore, brethren, by the mercies of God, that ye present your bodies a living sacrifice, holy, acceptable unto God, which is your reasonable service" (Rom. 12:1).

"MY ULTIMATE AIM"

It was my pleasure sometime ago to have a conversation with a distinguished philanthropist. I sought to find the motive which had prompted all of his excellent work. I said, in part: "You have aided in the erection of churches and hospitals; you have fed the hungry and cared for the poor; you have educated many young men and women. What is the motive that has prompted every act of yours along these lines?"

The sincere man answered, "My ultimate aim is to glorify Christ." He then explained that he did aid in the erection of churches and hospitals and have a part in other benevolent enterprises, and that every act of his looked to leading souls to Christ that they might glorify him. He then said: "I love Christ, and know that he is worthy of glory. Every soul won is another voice to praise him." This should be the ultimate aim of all Christians.

The prophet of Patmos wrote, "After this I beheld, and, lo, a great multitude, which no man could number, of all nations, and kindreds, and people, and tongues, stood before the throne, and before the Lamb, clothed with white robes, and palms in their hands; and cried with a loud voice, saying, Salvation to our God which sitteth upon the throne, and unto the Lamb" (Rev. 7:9-10).

NOT GOOD ENOUGH FOR JESUS

Out of our large family, growing up back yonder in the quiet hills so close to nature and to nature's God, it would seem right for God to call at least one to go to some foreign field to proclaim his glorious gospel. That is what he did, and for years one of my older brothers was one of our most faithful missionaries.

The missionary brother had made preparation in faithful work in public school, college, and the theological seminary. The Foreign Mission Board had made the appointment to China, the field of his choice. The young lady who was to be his life's companion had been appointed also. They were to be married, and then off for the long journey and years of service.

Our family desired to have a reunion at home on the last day the missionary brother could be there before leaving for China. He was to be married in south Georgia

the day before and arrive at home with his bride at ten
o'clock on the morning of the day of the reunion. All the
children were to be at home for this day. It was my
pleasure to go home the day before the reunion and assist
in perfecting plans for the occasion. Things had gone well,
and everything was as nearly ready as could be at that
hour for a perfect celebration.

Very early in the morning we began the final prepara-
tions for the day. Mother was on the back porch, weeping
as she worked. Seeing this, I went and sat by her side to
comfort her. "Mother," I said, "this is the last day Brother
will spend at home for many years. He has made his
decision to spend his life in China in the ministry of
Christ. It is right. He is happy in it. He may never
come back; and if he does, some of us may not be here.
Let us brace up today and give him courage for his work;
then we can weep after he is gone."

Mother then said, "I am not weeping because he is going."

"Then why do you weep?" I asked.

She replied immediately, "I wish I could do something
for him in getting him ready to go and in making his home
comfortable when he gets there."

Mother did not have the material riches of this world.
I turned the conversation to another side of the matter
by saying: "Mother, you have done everything for him.
You gave him birth. You cared for him in childhood.
You made it possible for him to have years of training and
to be able to go out for Christ. You have done everything
to get him ready to go."

Mother then dried away the tears from her eyes and
said, "Well, maybe I have done more for him than I think."

Then I drew close to her and said, "Mother, don't you think he is the best boy you have?"

Her reply was immediate and earnest, "All my boys are good boys, but the best I have is not good enough for Jesus."

I have said a thousand times since that morning, "Oh, for a million mothers in our land who feel that the very best they have is not good enough for Christ and his cause!"

"Worthy is the Lamb that was slain to receive power, and riches, and wisdom, and strength, and honour, and glory, and blessing" (Rev. 5:12).

6

Efficiency

Some years ago, when I was in Howard College, biology was one of my most interesting courses of study. In this particular class the students were required to draw likenesses of the magnified forms of the minute creatures which were studied, such as fleas, flies, gnats, etc.

My hands had been using farm tools most too long to be very skilled at such a task. Thus my drawings were not very neat. Too, there was an air of carelessness about the whole work.

So, when my drawings had been completed in that half-hearted manner, I carried them to the professor. He was busy at his desk, but turned aside to receive the drawings. After he had looked them over, he tore them into a thousand pieces, threw them into the wastebasket, and went about his work without even looking at me.

That action on his part was most peculiar to me. It puzzled me, and I stood for a moment not knowing what to do. But, to make sure of my position, I ventured to say to him, "Well, professor, that completes the work, does it?" He did not so much as look up at me, but pointed to the wastebasket and said, "That's finished! You get out of here and do that work!"

It dawned upon me then that the work had to be done,

and I was somewhat impressed that it might have to be done right. So I went again to the microscope to make another effort to draw the tiny things. Some hard work was done this time. Many hours, and even days were used in preparation of the drawings, and I took some little pride this time in presenting them to the teacher.

The professor was found at his same desk and in the same position in which I had found him on the former occasion. The work was presented. He received it cautiously, scanned it carefully, and again cast it into the wastebasket. The moment was serious with me. Like a big, overgrown, embarrassed, country boy, I cried a little that time.

When the professor heard the sniffing, he turned to me, pointed his finger into my face and said, "Look here, young man, you are not going to graduate from this college until you do your best on this work! Do you get it?"

I said, "Yes, sir, I think I get it!"

Then away I went to the city of Birmingham for the very best paper, the best drawing material, and the very best pencils that could be bought. At the best hour of the day I went to the laboratory, found the very best microscope, arranged the very best specimens of the tiny creatures, and this time did my dead level best at the job. I put every gnat's heel where it should have been. I put every flea's beard in place. The creatures appeared perfectly natural.

I was so absolutely sure that the work was just right and that the teacher would accept it this time that I went to the city again and had the drawings bound in black leather, and had my name in gold letters placed across the front of the booklet: Jerome Oscar Williams.

With fear and trembling, the little volume was placed on the desk of the professor. When he opened the book, a smile started on the end of his nose, played about over his face, and soon leaped off his ears as he began to view the work. Not much time was spent looking over the booklet. After he had gone through it, he placed it on the table before him and smiled, looking at me.

As the teacher began to remove his nose glasses, he said, "Well, Williams, that is not the best you can do, but," and I abruptly broke in and said, "But what? Are you going to 'but' it out again?" I stood there seemingly seventeen years waiting for that man to get his glasses into the case and in his upper, outside coat pocket. When finally the act was over, he relieved the tension by saying, "That's not the best you can do, but I suppose I will have to accept it." What a burden rolled off my heart!

Some of the drawings were not good, but the lesson which that experience taught me was more valuable to me than any I learned through my entire time in public school, college, and seminary. It was the lesson of doing my very best at everything. My best may not be even good for others, but for me it is my best, and the Lord will ever bless it if done for his glory.

From that time until now I never make an address, preach a sermon, visit a home, pray with the sick, plead with a sinner, or live a day without asking myself when it is over, have I done my best?

"She hath done the best she could," or, "She hath done what she could" (Mark 14:8) were the complimentary words of Jesus to the woman who anointed his body for burial. If we do this, we shall hear in the end, "Well done, good and faithful servant; thou hast been faithful over a few things, I will make thee ruler over many things: enter thou into the joy of thy lord" (Matt. 25:23).

"WE KNOW HOW"

Some years ago there was organized in Louisville, Kentucky, a new company for the purpose of packing, moving, handling, or storing household furniture and goods. This company now operates many very large vans in the city and to many parts of the country. All the vans are painted yellow, and in large black letters across the front is the motto of the company, "We Know How." From all accounts of the work of the company, it lives up to its motto. The company knows how to do the things for which it is organized.

This motto led me to asking questions. Would it not be great if all parents in the land could look into the faces of their children and say, "We Know How." How excellent it would be also if all teachers in the land could go into their schoolrooms and, in the spirit of this motto, have a conscientious desire to teach and train their pupils in a way to inspire them to attain their best.

What great progress the kingdom of God would make if every pastor in the nation could go to his church being taught of God and thoroughly able to say, "I know how to evangelize, to organize, to train, to teach, and to preach for the glory of God! Would that our churches had written in the very heart of every move, "We Know How" to lead to Christ the lost of the land and to build great, strong Christian characters! Blessed confidence when people can say, "We Know How," and then apply this knowledge in the most efficient and effective service in his kingdom!

"One thing I know (John 9:25); "one thing I do" (Phil. 3:13).

7

Faith

CLOSE TOGETHER

Our telephone rang early in the morning of Saturday, December 3, 1949. When I lifted the receiver and answered, a voice replied, "I'm Julian Hart, Jr., over on Hemingway Drive here in Nashville. I operate a short-wave radio set, and I have a contact in Asuncion, Paraguay. Your friend, Dr. Franklin Fowler, is standing by there and desires to talk with you."

He then explained that it would be a one-way conversation. He would make the connection, and Dr. Fowler would talk for a time, then he would change the direction and we could reply and make any further conversation.

The connection was made, and I heard and recognized the voice of Franklin as clearly as if he had been in the room with me. Then my wife and his wife had a visit.

No, I do not understand how it happened. In fact, it is hard to believe that it did. But it did! And it happens every day. Out of thin air, electrical energy spins a thread of sound to be tied here and there by the attention of men.

Such means of communication can draw the whole world very close together and place us next door to everybody. This should make it easy for Christians to carry out the commission of Christ, "Go ye therefore, and teach all nations, baptizing them in the name of the Father, and of the Son, and of the Holy Ghost: teaching them to observe all things whatsoever I have commanded you" (Matt. 28: 19-20).

HIS EYES SEEMED TO SAY

There is much in the look of the eye. The eyes speak. The expression on the face is an index to the soul. There is a look from the soul as well as from the eye.

On a cold Sunday morning in November many years ago, I was walking north on Fourth Avenue in Louisville, Kentucky, on the way to an interurban car going into Indiana, to meet an appointment for the day. It was already cold, and seemed to be getting colder every minute. The wind was brisk and sharp.

At the corner of Fourth Avenue and Jefferson Street a poor man had been placed on the sidewalk by a building, early in the morning, that he might receive alms from those who passed that way. The man was poor indeed. Both of his arms were gone; his legs were gone; his face was marked with miseries of many winters; but his eyes were bright. His head was bare, for his hat was pinned to his ragged but warm clothing.

An attempt was made to speak to him to know if he desired to be moved to the inside of the building. At the third effort to make him hear, one standing near by said, "He cannot hear."

"May I move you to a warm place?" was then written on a piece of paper, and, as it was placed before his face, the one standing near said, "He cannot read; neither can he speak."

Ways of communicating with the man were completely exhausted, it seemed. I could stand by, wonder, and say, "Poor fellow."

Looking upon him, his eyes immediately met mine, and his earnest look seemed to say, "O man! Please give me something with which to get bread, and a warm place to stay!" His look was so earnest, so intense, so pleading that it reached my heart. And since where a man's heart is, there is his treasure also, his look reached my purse, and he was helped to the extent of my ability.

The look of this man was from the physical eye. It was a pleading look, begging for the material things of this life. The look accomplished its purpose. The look was rewarded.

There is a more sublime look. The Lord God says, "Look unto me, and be ye saved, all the ends of the earth: for I am God, and there is none else" (Isa. 45:22). It is the look from the eye of the soul to the face of the Father for life eternal. This is the look that must be evident in the spiritual eye of every lost soul. It will bring its reward of life and love, joy and peace, grace and goodness, and faith and fellowship.

HOLDING HANDS WITH HEAVEN

The day had been very warm and an unusually busy one for me. I had gone home from an evening meeting and had gotten comfortable to rest awhile. The telephone rang, and when I answered, a voice at one of the hospitals requested me to come quickly to see a dying man and his grieved, sorrowing family.

I went immediately, and, when I arrived at the room,

I saw the father on the hospital bed in the throes of death. He was in agony. Three daughters, one son, one son-in-law, and one daughter-in-law stood about his bed with hearts breaking from grief. On inquiry, I found that the man was a good Christian, more than eighty years of age, and that there was no hope for his recovery.

I then said to the the members of the family, "The only thing we can do now is to pray the Lord to give him dying grace and to comfort our hearts in his going." Three members of the family stood on one side of the bed and three on the other side, holding hands with father and with each other, and I stood at the foot of the bed to complete the circle.

We prayed earnestly for a manifestation of God's grace just then for the dying man and the grieving family. Very soon, all pain left the man, rest came, eternal rest came, for quietly and quickly, with a smile on his face, the father went into the hand of the Lord that was stretched out at that hour for him.

God answers prayer. He gives dying grace. He gives comfort to the grieved.

"Behold, the Lord's hand is not shortened, that it cannot save; neither his ear heavy, that it cannot hear" (Isa. 59:1).

"Thou shalt also be a crown of glory in the hand of the Lord, and a royal diadem in the hand of thy God" (Isa. 62:3).

HOLD THE THUNDER

It was my pleasure to have a talk with a fine boy, age ten, about the salvation of his soul. He was most responsive and willing to talk about Jesus, his ability and readiness to save him, and about his faith in Jesus. He was direct in his answers to all questions, and it was soon seen that he had already trusted the Lord to save his soul.

After our conversation in the presence of his Christian mother, she said, "Now, may I have a word to say about him and his simple faith in the Lord?" She then continued in words like these: "He has always thought of the Lord as a constant companion, one to whom we may always go and talk as an allwise Father. I have always been afraid in a storm. One day the boy and I were out, and a bad thunderstorm came up. As we began to run toward the house, he said in all simplicity, 'Lord, hold the thunder till we get in the house!'"

Then the mother continued: "He had very beautiful curls when he was younger, and everybody greatly admired them. One day a stranger came by the house and stopped to talk with him. The stranger was admiring the curls, and said to him, 'I should like to have some beautiful curls like you have.' The boy answered in all faith, 'Ask the Lord, and he will give them to you.' Now, his simple faith in God has led him to trust the Lord for salvation, and I believe he is saved and ready to follow Jesus in baptism and church membership."

"For ye are all the children of God by faith in Christ Jesus" (Gal. 3:26).

"And a little child shall lead them" (Isa. 11:6).

"AH STAYS IN DE ATTITUDE"

"That which we have seen and heard declare we unto you, that ye also may have fellowship with us: and truly our fellowship is with the Father, and with his Son Jesus Christ" (1 John 1:3).

Some weeks ago, while waiting for a train at a small town, I fell into conversation with an elderly colored man. It was a bright and glorious morning. I said to the colored man, "Uncle, this is a wonderful morning, isn't it?" After hearing his hearty response, I said again, "We should thank the Lord for a great morning like this." This remark was the key to the good old man's heart. He replied in his characteristic language: "Yas suh, de Lawd am mighty good to us. He does things fo' us dat we cain't do fo' ourselves. Ah stays in de attitude of de Lawd."

Then, in the conversation that followed, I learned that he had been on the same job about that railroad station for a period of twenty years. He is a faithful, honest, energetic servant of the railroad. But a better thing about him: he has a family, a wife and children, and has ever done for them the very best he could. But, better still, he has become acquainted with the Lord, and he spends Sundays in his humble church and tries to be a good servant of the Lord. Thus, he could say, "Ah stays in de attitude of de Lawd."

How gracious it is that we can stay in the attitude of fellowship with the Lord and worship him continually! Jesus came to earth that he might reveal the Lord and his goodness to man. We have had that privilege, to learn of God the Father through him. We should so live that we can remain constantly in that gracious fellowship.

"If we walk in the light, as he is in the light, we have fellowship one with another, and the blood of Jesus Christ his Son cleanseth us from all sin" (1 John 1:7).

"LEAP OUT! THEY'LL SAVE YOU!"

One morning during my seminary days in Louisville, Kentucky, we boys were on the lawn in front of New York Hall just after breakfast. Some were singing songs, others having a friendly visit, and yet others leisurely enjoying the fresh air for a few minutes.

Suddenly the noisy, red fire wagons came rushing by. We looked in the direction in which the wagons were going and saw the smoke ascending rapidly from a building not so far away. Like all boys, we rushed away to the fire, some to be of help if possible, and others through mere curiosity.

When we arrived on the scene, we saw the Bush Sanatorium was burning from the center of the building. The firemen were rescuing the patients from the windows of the three-story building. Long ladders were extended to the windows, and strong firemen were bringing weak patients to safety. Stronger patients were climbing down ropes that had been securely fixed in the windows. All was excitement.

Alarming screams were heard from the rear of the building, and many rushed that way to find four men in great danger, begging someone to help them from the flames of the second story window. All ladders were being used. There were no other ropes. The fire was spreading, and something had to be done quickly to save the men from the horror of the flames.

Soon, four mighty firemen came with a strong net, and with one man at each corner, stretched it out beneath the window, braced themselves firmly, and cried to the men, "Now leap one at a time, and we will save you!"

One after another, three of the men leaped safely onto the net from the window and were sent away to another hospital. They trusted themselves bodily to the mercy and strength of the firemen. The way of rescue was safe. They were saved from the horror of the approaching flames.

The fourth man looked at the net and the men, and shook his head, saying: "I cannot risk that. Is there not some other way?"

The firemen replied: "The ladders are all being used elsewhere. There is no other way. This is safe. Leap out! We'll save you!"

But the man was not willing to risk it. He would not trust himself to the way provided for his safety. An impulsive friend of mine was near by nervously watching the procedure. Seeing the man being wrapped in flames, he could stand it no longer. He looked up at the man, threw his hands in the air and screamed aloud to him: "O man, leap out! Leap out of there! They'll save you! Leap out!"

The man would not risk the plan. He turned back into the burning building. Hours later, when the fire was under control and the building could be searched, the poor man's body was found, nothing but a burned, charred mass of dead human flesh. He would not risk the way.

The only way on this earth today for poor lost souls to

escape the fires of eternal punishment is by simple faith in the crucified Christ. The soul must trust itself wholly into the saving hands of Christ. It is the safe way. It is the only way.

"There is none other name under heaven given among men, whereby we must be saved" (Acts 4:12).

"Jesus saith unto him, I am the way, the truth, and the life: no man cometh unto the Father, but by me" (John 14:6).

RATHER DIE THAN DISOBEY

It was in the early part of November, 1918. We were in the First World War, and in the Battle of the Argonne. We had lost many men and, in fact, had not had time to find and bury the bodies and report the names to headquarters and to loved ones back home. Many parents in America became so anxious about their sons that they would call, wire, or write to their senators and have the senators to intercede for them to get some kind of information about their sons in the war zone in Europe. The messages would be sent to the headquarters of the divisions.

One day I was in the headquarters of one of the infantry units of our division, where I was serving temporarily in the absence of the regular chaplain. A little corporal from Division Headquarters came into our dugout, saluted the colonel, and said to him, "I have been commanded by the general to find out how many men in the territory over which you have command have fallen, and have not yet been buried and their names reported."

The colonel answered, "I do not know, sir," and pointed

to me, saying, "You might get the information from the chaplain."

The corporal then turned and saluted me and repeated what he had said to the colonel. I replied: "I cannot tell you. We cannot find all our dead in the nighttime, and we are commanded not to expose ourselves to death during the day in order to find and bury our dead."

The corporal answered as he stood at attention: "Yes, sir, but I am commanded to know. I must find out."

I answered, "Then there is just one way to do it; that is to go on the field and make a search for the dead bodies, and in the effort you will lose your own life."

The corporal stood for a moment as if he were dazed; then he saluted and said, "Sir, I will either find out, or I will die in the effort."

He turned and walked out of the dugout, up to the top of the hill, and over beyond. At the twilight of the evening, when we started out, we found that boy's body, just over the hill where it had been blown to pieces by shrapnel. A big sergeant looked at the pieces of his body as they laid them together, and said, "There is the example of a boy who would rather die than disobey his superior."

We often wonder if there is any soldier anywhere who would be truer to the uniform of his country than a minister of Christ, or a believer in Christ would be to the Lord Jesus Christ, his great Lord and Master.

The Lord said through John to the angel of the church in Smyrna, "Be thou faithful unto death, and I will give thee a crown of life" (Rev. 2:10).

WILL THE GATES BE OPENED?

Some weeks ago a young man who was not a Christian, in the world without God, without Christ, and without hope, was on his way to the city for an evening of revelry. Going down a hill, he lost control of his Ford. The car ran off the highway, down an embankment, and turned over on the young man. Later a passerby was able to get the young man from beneath the car, but found that his limbs were broken and that he had fatal internal injuries. He was rushed to a hospital, where he died in a few hours.

After his death I went to the bedside of his broken-hearted mother to see if I might be of some comfort to her. She wept bitterly as she grasped my hand, and looking into my face, she said, "It would not be so hard to give up his body, but, O my Lord, will the gates be opened?"

The gates of glory in the last day will be opened only to those who come to know Christ and accept him as a personal Saviour.

"Enter ye in at the strait gate: for wide is the gate, and broad is the way, that leadeth to destruction, and many there be which go in thereat: because strait is the gate, and narrow is the way, which leadeth unto life, and few there be that find it" (Matt. 7:13-14).

8

Guidance

ARROWS OF THE LORD

On a long drive through the country recently, we saw an unusual sign. It was a long arrow, possibly twelve feet long, swung by wire between two firmly-erected poles out in an open space, and it pointed over the highway and the mountains to the east. Written on one side of the arrow were the words, "Prepare to meet thy God," in large, bold letters. On the other side were the words, "Seek ye first the kingdom." We do not know who erected the sign, but certainly it makes a lasting impression on the people who see it.

The Lord has his arrows. The psalmist says, "O Lord, . . . thine arrows stick fast in me" (Psalm 38:1-2). The arrows may be in the form of sickness, loss of property, an earthquake, sorrow, or other acts of Providence. His arrows pierce the hearts of humanity. Many are now walking about with the arrows of God piercing their hearts every step of the way. No doubt the purpose of many of the arrows is that he may lead souls close to himself, "for whom the Lord loveth he chasteneth" (Heb. 12:6).

"GUIDE ME, MOTHER, GUIDE ME!"

A tragedy came to one of the homes of our church membership. There were four members of the family:

father, mother, daughter, and son, all Christians and members of the church. The seventeen-year-old son got in an automobile with a friend to go with him to his home across the city. On the way the automobile crashed into a streetcar and gave the youth fatal head and chest injuries.

Soon the boy was in the hospital, with the best medical care seeking to save his life. The family was about him, and the mother remained by his bedside through the dark hours of the night. We do not know just what the boy had in mind or the full meaning of his statement, but occasionally during the night he would raise his hands and voice and cry out, "Guide me, Mother, guide me!"

Thousands of boys and girls are looking into the faces of Sunday school teachers and saying by their attitudes each Sunday morning, "Guide me, teacher, guide me!" Thousands are looking into the faces of pastors as they seek to proclaim the message of the Lord on Sunday and are saying by their presence, "Guide me, pastor, guide me!"

What can we do? What shall we do? What a responsibility upon us! We cannot bear it alone. We can turn our hearts heavenward and say to the good Lord of all the earth, "Guide me, Lord, guide me!" Then we can hear him say, "I will instruct thee and teach thee in the way which thou shalt go: I will guide thee with mine eye" (Psalm 32:8). "And the Lord shall guide thee continually" (Isa. 58:11).

HE WILL LEAD US

Some years ago I was conducting a series of revival meetings in a small town in Tennessee. The Lord was blessing the services with great power, and the people had determined to seek the lost and try to lead them to Christ. Having preached that we must follow the leading of the Holy Spirit, it was then my duty to seek the will of the Spirit and follow him.

The morning service was over, and we had the noon meal and a few minutes' rest. Then, in a moment's prayer, I sought the Lord to direct me to someone to whom I might speak about his soul. Immediately the impression came that I should go to the ticket office at the railroad station and lead the agent to Christ. In another moment my steps were leading that way.

When I was within one hundred yards of the station, the agent came out and waved to me and said, "I knew you would come." When we had shaken hands, I said to him: "How did you know I would come. I did not call you. I sent no word. I made no engagement." "Yes," he said, "but I had an impression you were coming, and I am so glad to see you." By that time we were seated in his private office, and I could say to him, "Well, if you knew I was coming, you know also why I came and what I hope to do." He replied, "Yes, you are here to talk to me about my soul, and I am glad you came, for I need salvation."

We entered immediately into conversation about the power of the Lord to save a lost soul. He was requested to read certain verses of Scripture. While the man confessed his sin to the Saviour, the Lord saved him there and then. He made a public profession of faith in Christ at church that evening, followed Christ in baptism, joined the church, and has been faithful to Christ and his church through the years.

Yes, the Lord works at both ends of the line. If he impressed you that you should speak to another person about his soul, he also impressed the other person that you should. "He will guide you" (John 16:13).

"LO, I AM WITH YOU"

When my brother, James T. Williams, first went to China as a missionary, the person, Dr. Park Anderson, of Kentucky, who was to meet him and his wife at Hong Kong did not reach the port in time to greet them when they landed. They got off the ship, stood on the shore by the side of their baggage, looked first at each other, and then at the strange looking people. After a while, J. T. turned and looked at his wife. She was weeping, and he wept with her.

Then they decided to go up to what looked like a little hotel near by. They went to the building, found that it was a hotel, registered, went to a room, and had a prayer meeting, telling the Lord that they were at their row's end. He left his wife in the room and told her that he would go out and see what he could find.

As he left the hotel, a voice seemed to speak to him, "Lo, I am with you." He walked up the crowded street among the people of the foreign city with renewed faith and courage. At the end of the first block, he had an impression to turn right, and there, in the midst of the crowded street, moving hither and thither, he saw what he took to be an American. He wound his way through the crowds so that he could meet this person face to face.

When he met him, he said to him, "Sir, I do not know who you are, where you came from, where you are going, or what your business may be, but for my sake, I wish you would say a few words in good old American language." The man looked up into his face, extended his hand, and said, "My name is Park Anderson, and I am looking for J. T. Williams."

Until this day, you cannot change the opinion of my brother that the Lord was testing his faith the first hour that he stood on the soil of China. The Lord Jesus Christ promises his disciples, "Lo, I am with you alway, even unto the end of the world" (Matt. 28:20).

"MAKE ME SOME TRACKS"

During the cold, snowy days of winter, one of our friends from a southern city passed through our city of Louisville, Kentucky. At the railway station she called to tell us good morning. We insisted that she take a cab and come out to the house for a little while. When the driver came to the home, he stopped the car some feet from the end of the sidewalk where the snow had not been swept off. The young lady was wearing low shoes, with no rubbers, and she did not want to step in the deep snow. When we went out to meet her, she said, "Make me some tracks." The tracks were made, pressing the snow down, and she walked in the tracks.

Numerous people are looking to others today to make them some tracks. Children are looking to parents and saying: "Make me some tracks. Show me where to go.

I will follow in your tracks." Church members are looking
to leaders and saying: "Make me some tracks. Lead me
away from danger and into the path of true service."
Pupils are looking to teachers and saying: "Make me some
tracks. Show me the way upward and inspire me to go
therein." Voters of the land are looking to statesmen and
saying: "Make me some tracks. Lead me in the right and
just way of national affairs."

The great God of the universe has gone before us and
has made a way of righteousness, and now he seeks to lead
every soul in that upward and heavenly way. If we but
follow his leadership, he "shall set us in the way of his
steps" (Psalm 85:13), and we shall rejoice as we go singing along his glorious way.

WAITING FOR THE PILOT

Well do I remember the day, in 1918, when we were
just off the coast of war-torn France. As our ship neared
the shore, it began to slow down, and finally it came to a
stop. I remember asking one of the officers of the ship,
"Why are we stopping here?" His reply was, "We are
waiting for the pilot to come to conduct us safely into
the port." Soon the pilot came and conducted the ship
through the channel to the port, and the landing was successful.

This scene came back to me the other day as I stood
by the side of a dear, saintly soul. The question of how
much longer she might remain on the earth was the topic
of conversation. After a pause, the aged, saintly person

said, "I am just waiting for the Pilot to come to conduct me safely to port." Just a few days later, the Pilot came, and the soul of the saint went to be forever with Jesus.

> When at last I near the shore,
> And the fearful breakers roar
> 'Twixt me and the peaceful rest,
> Then, while leaning on Thy breast,
> May I hear Thee say to me,
> "Fear not, I will pilot thee."

"Though I walk through the valley of the shadow of death, I will fear no evil: for thou art with me" (Psalm 23:4).

"WE MUST BUILD"

A faithful minister of the Lord Jesus Christ accepted the pastorate of a church. He knew the building in which the church was meeting was inadequate for the work the church should do.

After the minister was well located on the new field and had won the confidence of the members of the church, he began to advocate the erection of an adequate church building. When the question was first mentioned publicly, the people said, "We suppose we should build."

The wise pastor then took the matter more seriously to the officers of the church, and, with the endorsement of some of them, the matter was mentioned again before the entire congregation, and the people went away saying, "We could put up a building."

The matter was kept before the congregation for a period

of time, and the minister preached on "Building for the Lord," and the people went away saying, "We can build."

By personal contact and public ministry, the conviction grew and began to take shape in the conscience of the people. All saw the need of a building and the ability of the membership to erect it. The interest grew in the hearts of the people until the time came when the pastor presented it again to the entire church, and, as one person, the members of the church arose and said, "We must build"; and they did, for the glory of Christ.

When we have that full-grown conviction about the work of our Lord, we Southern Baptists will stand as a man and say with the Lord Jesus Christ, we "must work the works of him that sent me, while it is day: the night cometh, when no man can work" (John 9:4).

"WHAT WE NEED NOW"

The little girls in our community had great pleasure with their paper dolls. From the magazines and catalogues they cut out paper houses and equipped every room with suitable furnishings. The living room, the library, the dining room, the bedrooms, all were thoroughly furnished with the paper furnishings.

When the house was thus thoroughly completed, they went to the task of placing a family in it. A little girl would first find a baby and all kinds of colors of clothing for it. Then the larger girl and the boy, with all the clothing, overcoats, and raincoats, would be put in place. When I inquired of the progress of the home, one little girl said, "What we need now is fathers and mothers." Paper people make poor parents anyway.

Surely this little girl said more than she knew about the present need of this world. We do need fathers and mothers who will store away in their hearts the eternal Word of God and then teach it diligently to their children. We need fathers and mothers who will be the right example in Christian living, in church and kingdom loyalty, and in leading the youth of the land to the highest development for Christ.

"These words, which I command thee this day, shall be in thine heart; and thou shalt teach them diligently unto thy children, and shalt talk of them when thou sittest in thine house, and when thou walkest by the way, and when thou liest down, and when thou risest up" (Deut. 6:6-7).

"YOU REMIND ME OF"

It was some years ago, in the city of Louisville, Kentucky. I was on my way up town about ten o'clock one morning. At Fourth Avenue, where I was to cross, there was much traffic. There was no traffic light, and the traffic officer had not come on duty.

While waiting to cross the street, I saw standing near me an old grandmother, leaning on her cane and pulling her glasses down, looking first east and then west on Broadway. I walked to her side and said, "Grandmother, do you want to get across the street?" She replied, "I do, but I go so very slowly that I fear the traffic will run over me." Then I said to her: "May I help you? If you will trust me, just put your hand on this strong right arm, and I will keep free my left hand to wave back the rushing machines, and I will see you safely across the street." She was happy to trust me. When we had crossed the street, and she had told me that she was going only to the corner drugstore, I bade her good day and turned to go along.

Grandmother's cane touched me on the back, and I turned to see if there was something else I might do for her. She motioned for me to come back, and she looked into my face and said, "Young man, are you a Christian?" I replied: "Yes, indeed, Grandmother. I am studying for the ministry. I live in New York Hall, and go to school over there in Norton Hall." Then she said: "Praise the Lord! I knew you were a good boy. You must have a good mother somewhere! I quickly said, "Yes, the best mother in the world!" She looked again into my face and said, "Do you know what you remind me of?" My reply was, "No, unless it be a tall, overgrown, country boy come to town." But she replied most seriously: "You remind me of the Holy Spirit." I said, "Please, Grandmother, do not compare me with one so high and holy." She said: "You have done for me just what the Holy Spirit desires to do for all Christians all the time. The Holy Spirit came into the world to walk along by the side of the Christian to keep away harm and danger, to lead in the path of right, to convict of sin, righteousness, and judgment, to testify of Christ, and to develop in us a full-grown Christian life for God."

9

Joy

In 1914 I visited Kentucky State Penitentiary at Frankfort. We went through the various factories and departments to see the prisoners and the work they were doing.

We came to one fine-looking young man who left an indelible impression on my life. He was neat, clean, energetic, courteous, and optimistic. He was performing the task before him with all cheerfulness, and smiled to the visitors who came his way. He had written on a large cardboard with his own hand, in beautiful letters, the motto of his life, "Keep Smiling."

We do not question the justice or injustice done to a man serving a term in prison. He was possibly getting what he justly deserved. But he certainly acted the part of a person whose sin had been covered by the One who has the ability to blot out all sin. He was a living example of the words of Ella Wheeler Wilcox:

It is easy enough to be pleasant,[1]
    When life flows by like a song,
But the man worth while is one who will smile,
    When everything goes dead wrong.
For the test of the heart is trouble,
    And it always comes with the years,
And the smile that is worth the praises of earth,
    Is the smile that shines through tears.

---

[1]Used by permission.

Surely, if a person in prison can live the smiling life, amid all the conditions that confront him, it should be possible for every genuine Christian with clean hands, pure hearts, noble purpose, and good conscience to live the optimistic, smiling life for Christ.

"Blessed is he whose transgression is forgiven, whose sin is covered" (Psalm 32:1).

STRIKE THE STRINGS GENTLY

One Sunday afternoon, some years ago, a message came to our home bringing sorrow. This message called for me to leave immediately after the evening worship service for a distant city to conduct the funeral of a loved one.

The night trip made it necessary to make a long wait in a dismal railroad station where we had to change trains. We were in the station from ten o'clock in the evening until after one in the morning. There were many others waiting for the same train. After the eleven o'clock train had gone by, the people waiting for the late train sought to make themselves as comfortable as possible for the remaining hours.

The night was cold, dark, and dismal on the outside, and not so much better within. In my own heart there was sorrow upon sorrow. The time seemed to drag by slowly, all too slowly for me. But soon something happened that made things different.

About the time that dull, drowsy feeling had well settled on the life of each one in the room, an insignificant looking young fellow came quietly in the room bearing a little old banjo under his arm. He found a seat near the center of the room, drew that instrument across his lap, and began to strike the strings gently. Soon, in a mere whisper, and with undreamed of harmony, he began to sing "Nearer, My God to Thee." When this old hymn had been finished, he moved into another great hymn and sang "Rock of Ages." Then, as if the instrument had been tuned for that very music, he glided softly into the old hymn, "Abide with Me."

How the atmosphere of that room changed! The sleepers aroused themselves and gathered about the musician. Smiles took the place of frowns. Joy took the place of sorrow. Light took the place of darkness. The moments went swiftly by while music cheered every heart.

The psalmist says, "O come, let us sing unto the Lord: let us make a joyful noise to the rock of our salvation" (Psalm 95:1).

SWEETEN UP A BIT

It was my pleasure to be a member of the faculty in a preacher's school in one of our churches. Real school work was done morning, afternoon, and evening, closing the day with an inspirational message in the evening for the people of the school and community.

The good people of the community were taking care of those who studied in the school, giving lodging and breakfast in the homes, and the noon and evening meal at the church. They employed a large colored woman to do the cooking at the church. She could cook to a queen's taste.

While the school was in progress, we had a period of severely cold weather, colder than it usually gets in the South. Some grave difficulties were experienced with water pipes and heating plants. It was difficult to keep warm, and much more difficult to prepare meals for about fifty Baptist preachers.

On one of these cold mornings, the colored woman came to the church kitchen and found everything frozen—no groceries, no help, and very little encouragement. About the time she became well-fretted over the situation and began to scatter pots, pans, boxes, and buckets every way, it was time for me to pass that way to my classroom.

The entire situation could be sensed at a glance, and one could see that something had to be done to improve the situation. It occurred to me that I might help conditions by singing a song. I walked over to the window, looked out into the icy day, and began to sing as best I could that little melody,

> Keep sweet, keep sweet,
> This is the way to win the day,
> This is the only way.
> If you just keep sweet.

The good old sister turned toward me, looked intently as a smile began on the end of her nose and spread all across her black face. When the little verse was repeated and finished, she shouted with a loud voice, "Now, parson, you's jest singin' dat to me, and I'se gwine sweeten up a bit!"

With a few other words of encouragement, I passed along to leave the sister to "sweeten up" and prepare the meal. She did, and we had the best dinner that day that she prepared during the entire time.

A song helps. There are many times in life when there is nothing that will so revolutionize conditions like a song. When things do not go right, sing.

A word of encouragement helps. There are thousands that are down and almost out, and a word of encouragement will bring them back, place them on their feet, and set them going in the right direction. Help the helpless. Encourage the discouraged.

An even temper helps. Little progress is ever made in anything while one is fretted and angry. Hold an even temper, and go forward in the right direction.

Jesus said, "In the world ye shall have tribulation; but be of good cheer; I have overcome the world" (John 16:33).

TOO HAPPY TO SPEAK

Many years ago I assisted pastor Fred M. Barnes in a series of revival services in Guntersville, Alabama. One evening an elderly woman came forward in the church to profess faith in Christ and to offer herself for membership in the church.

When the pastor shook hands with the woman, he sat down on the front pew and threw his hands over his face, as if he were in great pain. I went to him and said, "What's the matter with you, Fred?" He replied, "Go on away now; I'll tell you later." He wept, and rejoiced, and prayed.

After a time the pastor arose and said to the members of the congregation: "Folks, I'll have to ask you to forgive me tonight. My emotions have almost overcome me. I am too happy to speak. When I came here eight years ago, we took a census of this community, and found eighty-one people in the community over fifty years of age who said they were looking to this church for the way of life. I put those names in this little book, and promised the Lord that I would pray for each one of them everv day until the last one of them had accepted Christ as Saviour. I've been true to my promise, and the Lord has been good. This is the last one of the eighty-one. I've seen every one of them come to Christ."

No wonder he was too happy to speak! "The effectual fervent prayer of a righteous man availeth much" (James 5:16).

WHEN THE HEAVENLY FATHER FORGIVES

There is usually a time in the lives of boys and girls when they know more than their fathers or mothers, or when they think they know more than their parents. Whether this be true of everyone or not, it was true in the life of the writer.

It was one Sunday morning during this particular period of my life that I had a desire to do a certain thing. It was not wrong in itself, and no great harm would have been done. But when I asked Father if I might do it, he replied, "I don't believe I'd do that today." But I knew better than he, and said to myself, "I believe I will," when no firmer answer than that was given, and I did.

All day long, my conscience was telling me that I was doing wrong to go against the will of my father in that way. The day was not at all pleasant. Time was dragging. The hours went by all too slowly. When the sun was finally down, for I could not face the family in the light, I made my way homeward. When darkness had covered the earth, I went in the back way, to find that the family had already eaten the evening meal. Mother came, like a good mother does, and prepared my meal and placed it on the table.

As I sat down to eat, I heard heavy footsteps approaching, and Father came in and sat at the end of the table. I knew something had gone wrong. His face showed marks of pain; his hands were trembling. He looked at me and said, "Son, you have hurt the heart of your father today."

I could not eat then. All hunger had gone from me. I arose and went out on the porch. When father came out there, I left and went down in the orchard. Soon I returned and went to bed, saying, "I'll sleep to get relief from a guilty conscience."

When in bed, I could not sleep. Sleep had gone from my eyes. I arose and went to my father and said, "Father, I am sorry I have gone against your will today."

I can almost feel the strong arms of my father about me now as he drew me near him and said: "Son, I forgive you. Do not do it again." What a burden rolled off my heart! What a joy came into my soul! What a calm came over my life as Father spoke words of forgiveness!

If this great joy comes when an earthly father forgives our wrongdoings, what a supreme joy comes when the heavenly Father forgives our sin, and saves our soul for all eternity! The joy then is unspeakable and full of glory.

There's a song of joy, I sing it every day,
    For my every sin the Lord has washed away;
Trusting in His word, I yield to His Control,
    Since the loving Jesus saved my soul.

10

Life

"I AIN'T MUCH—HOW IS YOU?"

For years, in other days, we had our laundry done by a washerwoman. I would take it to her home on Monday and go back for it on Friday. On Monday morning, when I would knock at her door, the old woman would answer from within with much reluctance, and when I said "Good morning, Auntie! How are you this morning?" she invariably replied with the sad frown of blue Monday on her face, "I ain't much. How is you?" Then, when I returned on Friday, the week's work was over, and she was on the front porch waiting for the money to come in. As I handed her the ample pay for the work, I usually said to her: "How are you, Auntie?" She would answer with a smile, "Nicely, thank you! How is you?"

Had you ever thought: It is the same in the Christian experience? Before one is regenerated, given a new heart, a new life, a new purpose, a new hope, and new outlook on everything, he would have to say, "I ain't much." There are worlds of people all over this country who are not much. In the Christian realm, they are nothing, and not much of that. They do not live; they only exist. They have no aim in life, no end to attain, no service to render, and no motive for existence. Just nothing.

But when the powerful Christ comes and makes over the life, sends the person out with a new life, a new heart, a new hope, a new song, a new motive for living, and a zeal to work for the Master, he can answer every time, "Nicely, thank you." Service is now a joy, life is worth while, and he cheers all with whom he comes in contact.

How the world needs people who have been made over! People who are somebody, people who count for something, people who have zeal for the Master and serve with inspiration and eagerness for the advancement of his kingdom.

"I can do all things through Christ which strengtheneth me" (Phil. 4:13).

"MOST EVERYBODY KNOWS ME"

Some years ago, I was traveling on a small local train through a hill section of our country. The train would stop at every crossroad and every pole pile. At most every place a passenger would get on or off the train. It was most interesting to see the coming and going and to hear the remarks of each person.

At one little station an unkempt mountaineer came walking into the coach. He took a seat on the opposite side of the aisle from me and three seats in front of me. His clothing was ragged and soiled, his hair was long and unkempt, and his beard was filled with evidence of much use of tobacco. Yet, with it all, there was an effort on the part of the man to impress the people that he was some important personality. A few more stations down the way another character of the same type came drifting into the train. His eyes were immediately fixed on the person already seated, and when they were face to face, the man standing said to the other, "Hain't I seed you afore?"

The man then arose, looked into his face, and said: "I guess you have. I have been about a lot. I've been down to —————— (ten miles away) and up to —————— (fifteen miles away). Most everybody knows me!" He thought well of himself.

The man's language and appearance gave him away, and reminded all near by that the words of Paul in Galatians 6:3 would well apply to him: "For if a man think himself to be something, when he is nothing, he deceiveth himself." He also said, as recorded in Romans 12:3, "For I say, through the grace given unto me, to every man that is among you, not to think of himself more highly than he ought to think; but to think soberly, according as God hath dealt to every man the measure of faith."

"OUR TEMPER GETS AWAY"

Some years ago I was out visiting the membership of our church. I was on one side of a block, and desired to visit a family across the block. Since there were not many houses in the block, I simply went through the block, in order to save time and steps, and came up to the back of the home. The mother and her four children were on the back porch, and just as I walked up, before they observed me, the mother grabbed the largest son, gave him a mighty shake, and cried, "You little —————— !"

Then, as she took her eyes off the boy, they fell on me, and I said to her, "Mother, if your child is a little devil, then you are a big one, for you are the mother of the child." How terrible! There I was, an uninvited guest in the back yard of a home, and had called the mother a devil in the presence of her four children! I actually wanted the earth to open up and swallow me down. But it was too late then.

The mother was very much disturbed at her action and began to cry. Then she said, "I am sorry, Brother Williams." And when my mouth opened again, I made things worse by saying, "Are you sorry you said it or sorry that I heard you say it?" She answered "I am sorry I said it."

The mother then invited me to visit with them on the porch, and as we sat down, she took the child in her arms and, sobbing aloud, said: "My child is not a devil; he is an angel. I am so sorry I said it. Son, won't you forgive me?" The little fellow threw his arms about her neck and said, "Yes, Mother, I forgive you."

Then, turning to me, the mother said, "You know, Pastor, we mothers have all we can bear in the rearing of the little ones, and too often our temper gets away from us and we say too much. Will you ask the Lord to forgive me?" I replied, "I will ask the Lord to forgive you if you will." We had a prayer meeting there on the back porch. That mother then said, "The Lord being my helper, I will never say that again."

"Cease from anger" (Psalm 37:8). "Put off . . . anger" (Col. 3:8). "He that is slow to anger is better than the mighty; and he that ruleth his spirit than he that taketh a city" (Prov. 16:32).

THE DESIRE TO LIVE

A visit was made to the home of a woman who was in great physical, mental, and spiritual agony. The doctors had told her that quiet rest was absolutely necessary, and that without much rest it might be that she would never be well again. It was soon found that the mental and spiritual agony was far more severe than physical suffering.

The sick woman made a statement in words like these: "I do not fear death, but I want to live. I am not afraid to die, but I want to live. I am now more than fifty years of age, and I want to live at least twenty years longer. I could bear to suffer without a complaint for an entire year, but I do want to live."

Yes, the desire to live is as deep in every soul as life itself. No one really wants to die. We want to live. The way to live forever is to accept the Lord Jesus Christ and trust him wholly, and life will be eternal. Jesus said, "I am the resurrection, and the life: he that believeth in me, though he were dead, yet shall he live. And whosoever liveth and believeth in me shall never die" (John 11:25-26). "He that believeth on the Son hath everlasting life" (John 3:36).

With this firm faith in Christ, physical death is but a step into the unspeakable glory of the fulness of life with Christ and all the redeemed saints of all ages.

TO LIVE WITH JESUS

Out of all the men that I saw die during World War I, not one did I see who really wanted to die. One morning, on the front line, I came upon what I first took to be a discarded blanket, overcoat, or uniform, but I found it to be the mangled body of one of our soldiers. Shrapnel had left his body with every limb broken, and other wounds on his body. He was dying in his own blood there on the battlefield. When I came to him, I saw that he was still breathing. I placed my hand on his forehead, and with the husky voice of death, he whispered for water. I gave him water from my canteen, although I knew he could live but a short time.

When he had drunk the water, he revived for a moment, looked up into my face, and said, "Chaplain, do you think I can live?" I answered, "No, my boy, I must be true to you: you cannot live. Your limbs are gone, your blood is gone, and your life is fast going." He then looked at me and said, "I do not want to die." Then I replied, "No, no one wants to die; we want to live."

Then, with a smile on his face, he said, "Well, I guess if I cannot live here, I can live on the other side." I assured him that he could live on the other side if he had made it all right with the Lord. He answered: "Long time ago, back in old Missouri, I settled that matter. You can write to my mother and tell her that I am going home to live with Jesus."

"And if I go and prepare a place for you, I will come again, and receive you unto myself; that where I am, there ye may be also" (John 14:3).

TOO BIG A HURRY

Recently an old colored man in central Kentucky drove a faithful team of mules eight miles into town to get a ton of coal. After he had loaded his coal and started back home, it began to rain. But, in his raincoat, he rode along the asphalt highway with all ease and satisfaction. People all over the country knew the old man as "Preacher." Along the highway, as he returned, he gave the team ample time, as he possibly communed with himself, his team, nature, and had fellowship with the Lord of all nature.

As he drove thus along the highway, our automobile started to pass him, but the driver saw another car coming from the other direction, and knew that we would not have time to pass. He tried to stop, but the highway was very slick, and the car skidded for several feet and ran into the back of the wagon. The wagon was knocked into the middle of the road, the coupling tongue was broken, and the good old man was thrown out on the side of the road. The team stopped immediately.

We got out of the car and came to where the man was. As he gathered himself together and got up out of the mud, in great excitement he demanded to know what had happened. When all was explained to him, he put his hands on his hips and said very deliberately, "I jes' guess all the world is in too big a hurry." We paid all damages, left him satisfied, and went on our way.

Perhaps the old man said more than he knew.

11

Love

"HOW WE LOVED HIM!"

We enjoy hearing about the good fortune of the people we love. When I came back to America after the horrible days of World War I, a mother and her family met me at the port city.

With eager hearts the family gathered about me as I opened my records to tell them all about one of their loved ones who had gone the way of death in the front line in France. They said: "We understand you buried our loved one over there. Please tell us about his wound, his death, and his burial." When the records were opened, memory began to work, and I told them all that I had written and all that I could remember about the boy.

How the sorrowing members of the family listened eagerly to every word I spoke as I told of his death in the field hospital and of his burial in a little cemetery in France, as the commanding officers and sorrowing comrades stood with bared heads. After we related the facts, there was a long silence as the members of the family grieved. The sister broke the silence, saying, "Oh, how we loved him!"

Just so, if we love Christ we will never tire of hearing the charming story of his wonderful life, work, and power. We will often gather in his house to honor him, to serve him, and to worship him. The charm of the pulpit has been, and will always be, Jesus. As we hear the story of his love over and over again, it will grow sweeter and sweeter, and our love for him will increase.

"And thou shalt love the Lord thy God with all thy heart, and with all thy soul, and with all thy mind, and with all thy strength: this is the first commandment" (Mark 12:30).

MOTHER'S LOVE, GOD'S LOVE

Some years ago I went into a small town to become pastor of the First Baptist Church. It was reported to me soon after my arrival that there was a family in the community with a child who was grown in years but whose body had never developed. The description of the person was so unusual that it aroused my interest. Before very long, one Sunday afternoon, all alone, I sought out the home and called on the family. As I approached the house, there were many children playing about in the yard, and older people on the porch. It was evident at first sight that this was the home of a very large family of children and that some of them were grandchildren.

As I came near the doorsteps, one of the young men arose and introduced himself to me; then he introduced me to the other members of the families present, and finally to his mother, who was sitting on the end of the porch. I sat down by the mother and with much interest heard her story of the large family and saw how her heart rejoiced to see the grandchildren playing with glee in the yard.

But no mention had been made of the child who had not grown. Very soon an opportunity came to me to say, "They tell me that you have a child that has never developed to maturity."

She rejoiced that I would inquire about the little fellow, and answered: "Yes, I have. Would you like to see him?"

We arose, and she conducted me into the hall and to a back room where, on a bed, was the most pitiful specimen of humanity that I have ever seen. She told me of his life, his name, and of her care for him for the forty-five years that he had been living.

My heart was greatly moved as I looked into the face of that child, so old. The hands were so weak that they had never been able to convey so much as one drop of water to his mouth. The face was void of any expression except a bare smile. The life was helpless, and seemed to be useless; and yet, I am sure it was not.

I suppose I asked the wrong question as we stood there over the child, for I said, "Mother, do you love this child as you love your strong children?"

When this question was asked, the mother lovingly caressed his little brow, her lips quivered, and great tears formed in her eyes as she replied, "I would be willing to die now if this child could have a strong body like my other children have."

When this poor mother yearned for her weakest, I said to myself, "Surely the love of a true mother for even the weakest of her children is the very best illustration of the love of God for all, even the weakest."

Not long after this, the child was taken seriously ill one day, and the family called me to the home. I went to pray for the mother and family, for we all knew that when the child should leave this world he would go immediately to be with Jesus.

The child died, and the next day we came to the home for a simple funeral service. The little body was carried with loving hands to be left in the final resting place.

When the new-made grave had been completed, and all were ready to leave, the mother cast herself on the mound and said: "I cannot leave him. All these long years I have never left him for one night. I cannot leave him now."

We tried to explain to the brokenhearted mother that she had ever been faithful to him while he was living and that she had done all that she could for him. All persuasion failed. Every plea was turned down. Finally, by force, the husband on one side and I on the other, we literally lifted her from the grave.

She returned home to suffer that awful void of having one gone from her heart and life. The sorrow was too great for her. In a few days she passed away of a broken heart, and her body was placed in a grave near the child for whom she had given her life.

Surely this love comes near to the love of God. "God so loved . . . that he gave." Yes, and because of the same love, Jesus gave his life on the cross that the world might through him have eternal life.

THE LOVE OF GOD

Some years ago I was passing down a street in the city of Birmingham. At the corner of Avenue F and Twenty-seventh Street, I saw a young man sitting on the curb, crying. I went to him and made several inquiries, seeking to learn his trouble and to help him. Every question was turned away with a bitter answer.

When I asked if he had a message of sorrow from mother, father, or home, he replied that he did not know that he had a living mother or father and that he had no home. He then turned to me and said, "Who are you?"

I explained, "I am a minister, and pastor of the church near by, and want to help anyone in trouble."

"Ah," said he, "that is different. I was coming down the street a few minutes ago and heard the voice of a girl singing a song with words like these:

> "His love for me! His love for me!
> High as the heavens, deep as the sea,
> His love, His love for me!"

"And I asked, 'Whose love?' And the reply came to me, 'God's love.' Then I asked, 'Who does God love?' And I was assured that he loves me. Preacher, I cannot see how God can love a sinner like me. I have done everything mean on earth. I have lied, stolen, committed every crime, and have gone under six assumed names. I am too mean for even God to love."

I saw that he was under deep conviction of sin. I took him by the arm and led him to my room. I gave him the best chair I had. When he was seated, I picked up the Bible and said, "Do you know what this is?"

He replied, "It is the Bible."

Then I said, "Do you believe it?"

And he said, "I don't know much about it, but I'm sure it is true."

I inquired if he could read. He said he could, and would believe what he could read in the Bible. I turned to John 3:16, and he read it. I then said, "Now, read it again and put your name in place of 'the world.' "

He looked at it and said, "I see what you mean," and started reading, "And God so loved," and he stopped again and looked up at me and said, "I guess I had better put my real name there."

I said, "Yes, put the name your mother gave you."

He then read, "God so loved James Robertson." He stopped and said, "How am I going to know he loves me?"

Then I told him to get on his knees and tell the Lord all the mean things he had done and ask him to forgive. The boy fell to his knees, confessed his sin, trusted the Lord, and arose a trusting and happy soul.

After urging him to shave and bathe and get dressed in a suit of my clothes, I went with him to the city for something to eat. As we walked down the street, he placed his hand upon my shoulder and said, "I feel like a new man." Then, with emphasis, he said, "I am a new man."

I inquired, "What makes you a new man?"

He replied, "The love of God."

How can any soul resist this eternal, compassionate love of God?

"But God commendeth his love toward us, in that, while we were yet sinners, Christ died for us" (Rom. 5:8).

THREE ROSES

I went to see a grandmother in our church membership who was ill. On my way to see her, I stopped at the florist shop and got three beautiful roses. When I arrived at the home, the roses were placed in an attractive vase, and I carried them to the room of the aged lady. The sight of the roses brought a pleasing smile, which was reward enough for me in this deed for Christ's sake.

The meaning was explained. These roses have a significance. This one is named *Faith*. This one is *Hope*. This one is *Love*. You may take this in at least two ways. It may mean our faith in you, our hope for you, or our love for you. We do believe in you, and hope for the Lord's richest blessings upon you, and express our love for you. Or you may express by these roses your faith in God, hope for the future, and your love for the Master and his church and kingdom. Only I remind you that the roses in their present state might express faith, hope, and love, for the roses will fade and wither, but never will His love for us fade.

What joy was brought to this lonely heart as the roses were presented! How graciously they were received and cherished! We serve Christ by doing lovely things for others in his name. How many times we fail to use every opportunity for him!

"But now abideth faith, hope, love, these three; and the greatest of these is love" (1 Cor. 13:13 ASV).

12

Missions

ENLARGE YOUR INTEREST

Sometime ago, in a meeting of the deacons, we were seated about the table discussing the work of the church. The question of support of all the causes fostered by the denomination came up. The Cooperative Program was well explained. One of the deacons finally said: "I think a member of the church should have the privilege of saying where his own money should be spent. Now take my case. I am interested in the Orphan's Home and also in the athletics of the church. I am willing to give my money for the support of these causes, but I am not at all interested in the rest of the program."

I immediately turned to him and said: "You need to enlarge your interests. The church does not attempt to do anything that should not be done. If all the things the church seeks to do should be done, and every cause is a worthy cause, then it is worthy of the support of every member of the church. The Cooperative Program of our denomination is so arranged that when a person gives a dollar to the cause, the money goes to support missions, education, and all of the benevolent causes of the denomination. It takes a larger Christian to support all causes than it does to support only one or two."

The deacon soon saw that it was an immensely larger thing to support the entire program of the denomination.

Herein is one of the greatest needs of the members of the churches in our country.

"Enlarge the place of thy tent, and let them stretch forth the curtains of thine habitations: spare not, lengthen thy cords, and strengthen thy stakes" (Isa. 54:2).

"I'M COMING AFTER YOU"

It happened back when hundreds of fine Baptist young men and women were in Newton Baptist Institute, of Newton, Alabama. Many of us would go out on Sundays all over the country to assist churches in missions, Sunday schools, Training Unions, rallies, and institutes.

Several of us had gone to Antioch Church, four miles south of Dothan, to assist in a Fifth Sunday Rally. Jesse Rogers, who later went to China as a missionary, was to speak on missions at ten-thirty one Sunday morning. Before the service, he filled the walls of the church with maps, charts, and placards. To show these to the best advantage, he had to have a pointer. Finding nothing about the church that he could use, he went into the woods to cut a stick for a pointer, and in cutting the small twigs off of it, he cut the stick almost in two.

When time came for him to speak, he arose, and, first of all, pointed out many things on the maps, charts, and placards. And then, with pointer in hand, he became very enthusiastic in making his speech on missions. In making one of his optimistic gestures, the pointer broke, and one piece just barely missed the head of a deacon and went on down the aisle of the church. The deacon arose quietly and started to hand it to him. Jesse exclaimed: "Let it alone, brother. I'm through with that now. I'm coming after *you*." He then went after the people who were not supporting a worldwide program for Christ.

Possibly one of our main troubles is that we do not first give ourselves to the Lord. If we did, he would then have our means for the support of his kingdom.

"But first gave their own selves to the Lord" (2 Cor. 8:5).

"I WANT TO GIVE THE LIGHT"

It was the week of instruction about missions and preparation for support in our church. The congregation assembled each evening. The work of the various boards of our denomination was presented in pageant form by a cast of fifteen or more characters.

When we came to Thursday evening, the work of the Foreign Mission Board was the subject of the pageant. A large candle was placed on the altar, and a small candle was given to each person who came to the service.

After the preliminary songs and prayers, all the lights were extinguished, and the large candle on the altar was lighted to give all the light for a time and to represent the light of Christ. Intense interest was manifested in every move of the service.

While the light was burning on the altar, eighteen girls dressed as nationals came bearing a small candle, each representing one of the countries in which our Foreign Mission Board is doing work. Standing in the light of Christ, each presented the facts about the country represented, told of its need of the light of Christ, and made an appeal for this light. Each then said, as she took her stand in the dark corner of the room: "We wait in darkness for the light of Christ. Please send it to us."

While these eighteen girls waited in darkness with un-lighted candles representing the unenlightened countries, the choir sang "Send the Light."

I then walked to the altar, lighted my candle from the large one, and said: "I now have the light of Christ. I wonder if the deacons of this church have the light of Christ." When this statement was made, each deacon present came forward and lighted his small candle.

I then said to the deacons, "Will you please assist me in giving the light to every person present?" The deacons went down the aisles lighting the small candle of each person on each end of the pews, who in turn gave the light to the person next to him, until every person in the church was holding high a lighted candle representing the light of Christ.

While this was being done, the choir sang most impressively:

> The morning light is breaking,
>   The darkness disappears;
> The sons of earth are waking
>   To penitential tears;
> Each breeze that sweeps the ocean
>   Brings tidings from afar,
> Of nations in commotion,
>   Prepared for Zion's war.

Then when every person in the building, except the eighteen lonely-looking girls representing the nations of the earth, was holding his lighted candle, the light of Christ, the choir sang brightly "Let the Lower Lights Be Burning."

I then called for volunteers to give the light to those who were waiting in darkness, representing the various nations. One of the good men of the church arose immediately and came down the aisle, saying, "I want to give the light of Christ to Africa," and he lighted the candle of the girl representing that nation.

A deacon of the church came with his heart full of the love of God and said, "I want to give the light of Christ to waiting Japan."

A good woman came weeping and said, "We've heard the call from distant China, and we must give the light of Christ to the Chinese." Men, women, and children came to indicate their willingness to give the light of Christ to the nations. Our little five-year-old daughter came to the altar with her lighted candle, saw that all candles of the girls representing the nations had been lighted, and said, with tears in her eyes and a tremble in her voice, "I want to give the light to some nation." All were moved profoundly to consecrate themselves to the task of giving the light of Christ to the nations of the world.

The candles were then extinguished, as the lights were turned on, and a prayer of consecration was prayed amid many sobs. We were inspired to take more seriously the Great Commission of Jesus as spoken to his disciples, "Go ye into all the world, and preach the gospel to every creature" (Mark 16:15).

PEANUTS, PINDERS

One of the great difficulties with most people is the lack of energy. Many were born tired, and they have never gotten rested. Yet, we do greatly admire the person who goes into his work with enthusiasm.

Sometime ago, I was on my way to a town in which one of our denominational colleges is located to conduct a series of revival meetings in the church there. It was necessary to change trains at a small village. Many people were getting off the train.

As we stepped off the train, an old colored man was standing almost in our way. Many marks of misfortune were all over his body. His form was stooped, one leg was shorter than the other, one hand was gone, his face was wrinkled, and his kinky hair was snowy white. Yet with all of this, he exercised remarkable energy in his work.

The old man was holding a small basket of sacked, parched peanuts on the arm that had no hand. As he shoved the basket into the faces of the travelers getting off of the train, he cried with great zeal, "Peanuts, pinders, goobers, ground peas! Eat 'em! Eat 'em!"

I said to the old fellow, "I do not care for your ware, but I greatly admire the zeal with which you boost it," and bought a package.

Other passengers were buying. They were all buying. Whether they desired the peanuts or admired the zeal of the salesman, they were buying. The zeal, energy, and enthusiasm of the old, brokendown colored man put the job over. He did the thing he was trying to do. He arrived. He accomplished. He was successful.

I looked at that old colored man and thought, "If that poor old Negro can put that much zeal into the small business of selling peanuts for five cents a bag, how much more enthusiasm should Christians put into the big business of preaching the gospel of Christ to the lost world!"

Enthusiasm is contagious. People like it. They will respond to it. It gains momentum in the going.

It will work in the pulpit. Billy Sunday was a good example of how it will work in preaching.

It will work in promoting and building large Sunday schools. W. C. Pearce, a prominent leader in international Sunday school work, was a man with consecrated zeal for the Lord's cause.

It will work especially well with young people, as demonstrated by Dr. L. P. Leavell, the first Southwide B.Y.P.U. secretary.

Of course, zeal, energy, and enthusiasm must be tempered with wisdom, knowledge, good judgment, and power from the Lord. It would be well if it could be said of every Christian that he is "clad with zeal as a cloke" (Isa. 59:17).

THE SOUND OF THE OLD BUGLE

It was years ago when we boys were growing up, far out in the country. The days were spent in hard work on the farm. At night there was only a brief time to read, and then to needed rest from the long day of labor. Saturday afternoon was ours for a ball game, fishing, stroll in the woods, or a visit to the home of a neighbor boy to spend the night. The Sundays were spent attending the Sunday school and the church services one time each month.

During these days, a hardware company in Selma sent out, at intervals, an old colored man with a covered wagon filled with tinware to supply the rural population. A big old bugle was carried on a rack by the cover of the wagon, and the driver, who was also the peddler, would use it to tell the people all over the country that he was in the community and that soon they might be supplied with tin cups, plates, buckets, spoons, etc.

I shall never forget, so long as I live, the first time I heard that old bugle sound. We boys were down in the "low field" chopping cotton on a hot May afternoon, about four o'clock. As usual, I was far in the rear of the other boys. The sound of that old bugle came rolling down that valley like a call to judgment. I immediately dropped my hoe, stood rigid like a marble statute, and said to myself, "There now, Gabriel has sounded his horn!" Visions of the end of time came to my young mind. I thought all work was over. I thought we were to leave immediately for the other side. After some moments, by the help of my older brothers, I came to myself, and gladly learned that it was only the tin peddler coming into the community.

We boys assembled in a group there in the field and talked and wondered for sometime. We again went about our work, and in just a few minutes that very wagon— mules, driver, tinware, bugle, and all—came down our lane going in the direction of our home. There was no more work for us that afternoon. We had an unquench- able desire to see the very spot from which all that noise had come. We ran to the house. When the man drove up to our gate, we begged Father to let him spend the night with the servants on the place. Father agreed.

All night long, I wondered if that bugle would be quiet until morning. All night long, I dreamed of that mighty instrument filling itself for another blast able to wake up the dead. In the early morning, I arose and peeped that way to see if a mighty blast of the instrument had not blown away the barn, only to see that it was exactly as it was left the evening before.

That morning, we were loath to leave the house for the field until that wagon was moved and a further investigation of the bugle was made. In fact, we could not leave! The curiosity of a boy had not been satisfied. His many questions had not been satisfactorily answered. It pleased us much when the old man appeared just after breakfast was over and went to the barnyard for his mules. The team was soon hitched to the wagon and standing in front of our gate, ready to go. After we made a small purchase of his ware, and just before he was ready to check up the reins of the team for the day, he said, "I suppose I had better tell the people I am coming."

We shall never forget those moments. We stood there almost in distress as the old colored man drew the rack around and adjusted the bugle for the blast. When all was ready, there pealed forth from that bugle mighty strains of music, almost enough to make the earth tremble, bidding a happy good morning to every household in that entire country. We had seen the act well done. We had heard the joyous sound, which had been a joy forever. The rack adjusted in its place, the old man bowed, tipped his hat, smiled a happy good day, and went on his journey.

It occurs to me that every church in the land should be like that old bugle. They should sound forth the glad tidings of the Christ to all the world round about. It was so with the church at Thessalonica, "For from you sounded out the word of the Lord not only in Macedonia and Achaia, but also in every place" (1 Thess. 1:8).

WHAT TO SCRAP

It happened in a great laymen's missionary conference. A good program had been prepared, and for three days, large numbers of men gathered to talk about the work of the kingdom in all the world. More than a thousand men were enrolled. Large numbers attended each session. Some very inspiring addresses were made.

The time came for conference on the methods of our boards in doing mission work, with Bishop Ainsworth conducting the conference. Questions came thick and fast from all parts of the auditorium. One earnest student of the great mission enterprise arose and asked, "Do you think our Board will have to scrap the present methods of doing mission work and get something new?" Bishop Ainsworth replied that it would not be possible to do away with all our methods but stated that perhaps they would have to be modified. He then closed his remarks on this question by saying, "We need to scrap this going to a million dollar church in a half-million dollars' worth of automobiles to drop a dime on the collection plate to Christianize the world." We are sure the bishop is right.

Materialism has gotten such a hold on American people that we spend far too much to gratify personal wishes and far too little for the advancement of the kingdom of God. We place emphasis on things that are perishable rather than on things that are eternal. We invest our treasures in things of the earth. "Lay not up for yourselves treasures upon earth, where moth and rust doth corrupt, and where thieves break through and steal: but lay up for yourselves treasures in heaven" (Matt.6:19-20).

13

Prayer

ACCORDING TO HIS WILL

Word came to me one morning that one of the good women of our church membership had been stricken with paralysis. We went to see her immediately and found that she was in a critical condition, having lost the use of one arm and one limb and being in great pain otherwise. It was the doctor's orders that no one go in to see her; but when she heard that her pastor was there, she wanted to see him, and the request was granted.

I stood by her bedside and talked quietly to her for a few moments. Soon the afflicted woman drew back the sheet with her good hand, lifted the useless one, and said, "Pastor, I want you to take this hand in yours and pray earnestly now that the Lord will heal it for me."

Deep down in my heart I said to myself: "I cannot do that. I can only pray that the will of the Lord may be done in the matter. The Lord knows best, and he has taught us to pray 'in his name' and 'according to his will.'" With the paralyzed hand in mine, I talked with the Lord and earnestly asked him to accomplish his will in the matter; and he heard and answered the prayer.

It should ever be the deepest desire of our soul to live so near the Lord that we can know his will, and then pray to him in accord with his way and will. Our vision is too limited, our life too small, and our way too earthly to have our own way when there is ever present an all-wise Father at our side to direct every move of life.

"This is the confidence that we have in him, that, if we ask any thing according to his will, he heareth us" (1 John 5:14).

BEGIN WITH PRAYER

When I was a student in Howard College, in Birmingham, Alabama, I was also pastor of Twenty-seventh Street Baptist Church. Two doors from me lived an engineer who operated one of those large passengers locomotives over the Southern Railroad to Atlanta, Georgia.

I told him once that I should like to go with him some morning to see him get ready to make his run. The time was arranged, and we were in the station some minutes before his engine came in from the roundhouse. When it arrived, he took his oil can and touched here and there as he explained many things to me, and said, finally, "She is in good shape this morning, and we should make the trip safely." Soon I lost the man, and I wanted to ask another question. Going to the other side of the great machine, I saw the man down on his knees by the great driving wheels, praying the Lord to give him a safe trip that day.

That is the kind of man I like to have at the throttle when I go on a trip by train. That is the way to begin all things. Begin every task of life in prayer, and pray it through.

"I will therefore that men pray every where, lifting up holy hands, without wrath and doubting" (1 Tim. 2:8).

BOYS CAN PRAY

It has ever been a pleasure in my ministry to be with the boys of the church and community where I have been pastor. They are the men of the future, the fathers of the future, and the leaders of the future. Thus, in the Boy Scout movement and other organizations for boys, I have taken a great delight and have tried to be helpful.

Many years ago it was my pleasure to have about me a fine group of boys of the church. One evening we were together for a delightful social meeting. When the meeting was over, I said to the boys, "Suppose we have a prayer before we go home."

When the question of prayer was mentioned, some of the boys were just a bit shy. They looked at one another with a look that seemed to say, "Who in this crowd can pray, except the preacher?"

But while the boys were nudging and winking at one another, I was busy arranging some small chairs so that we might be seated in a circle. When we were all seated, the boys were informed that each one would be expectd to take part in the prayer.

This announcement confused the boys for a moment. Then one of the young fellows was requested to tell us what he would pray for if he just knew that the Lord would give it to him at that time. When the request was made, there came a serious look on the face of each one.

Soon the boy began his reply: "I would ask the Lord to save my grandmother. You know she is very sick. We think she will die. I love my grandmother, and I like to go over to her house because she loves me and always treats me so well." By the time the answer was made, there was a most serious look on the faces of all, and they were interested and sincere.

Then another boy was requested to tell us what he would pray for if he knew the Lord would answer his prayer. He began most seriously: "You know my mother is very ill, and the doctor said this morning that he did not know if she would get well. I would ask the Lord to make her well. I do not know what we would do without Mother."

When the third boy as to tell us the thing that was most desired in his life, he said: "You know my father is a bad man. He comes home drunk and beats Mother and the children. We are all afraid of him. I wish he could be a Christian like Uncle William. I would ask the Lord to save my father and make a good man out of him."

The fourth boy said: "I would ask the Lord to bless me and help me to be a good and useful preacher. I love the Bible now, I love the Lord, and I have accepted Christ as Saviour and joined the church. I try to be good, and I want to be useful and help folks everywhere." Another boy said: "You know I am not a Christian. I would ask the Lord to save my soul."

The same course was pursued until every one of the nine boys had mentioned the thing about which he would pray to the Lord. We all then bowed our heads, and this group of boys, who thought a few moments before that they could not pray, were soon in earnest petition to the Lord for the blessings that were uppermost in their hearts.

The marvelous thing about this prayer meeting was that the prayer of every boy was answered almost immediately. The grandmother and the mother both recovered from illness, and are living now. The sinful father became a Christian in only a short time. The boy who prayed to the Lord for the salvation of his soul was saved on the following Sunday.

Everyone can pray. Sinners can pray for forgiveness, and Christians can pray for themselves and others.

"Lord, teach us to pray" (Luke 11:1).

"The effectual fervent prayer of a righteous man availeth much" (James 5:16).

CRY MIGHTY LOUD

When our convoy of ships landed their cargo of troops in France, I was assigned to Camp I at Saint-Nazaire as camp chaplain. This was the camp where the troops were landed and remained for only a short time before going on to the interior and on to the front.

In one section of the camp there were about six thousand Negro troops who served as laborers in the port. They worked in shifts. Two thousand worked while the same number slept, and the same number idled about the camp. It was my pleasure to go down to the Y.M.C.A. hut and preach to more than a thousand of these fellows at morning, afternoon, and evening. When I preached at the evening hour, there was always a large, coal-black fellow named Jim on the front row who wanted a part in the service. I usually called on him to pray. He would pray along earnestly for a time, bowing low on his knees, with his face near the floor. About half way through his prayer, he would straighten up, look toward heaven, and cry for the Lord three times, just as loud as he could scream. He would then assume his former position and go along.

One evening, after the service in which he had led the

prayer, I heard another Negro say to him, "Jim ah wants to ax you som'n." Jim said, "What you wants to ax me, Sam?" "Ah wants to ax you why you cries so loud to de Lawd. Don't you know he can hear you widout you yellin' to him like dat?" said Sam. Jim replied, "Go on way fum here, Sam! De Lawd am a long ways fum dis here place, and ah has to cry mighty loud fur him to hear me."

There are many white people who believe that the Lord is far away. Yet, how mistaken! "He be not far from every one of us: for in him we live, and move, and have our being" (Acts 17:27-28). "The eyes of the Lord are in every place, beholding the evil and the good" (Prov. 15:3).

PLEASE PRAY

A letter came to me one morning from a young woman. She said: "I am making a decision today that will affect all the rest of my life. Please pray that my decision may be right in the sight of God."

The next morning a young man came into my study trembling and all upset, and said: "Pastor, I'm all undone this morning. I want you to pray for me. I'm in grave distress, but cannot tell you now. Please pray for me." We prayed together, and the Lord helped him to solve his problem.

The next day had gone by, and late in the evening the telephone rang, and a voice said, "Will you please come to the Baptist hospital and pray with my sister and me while mother passes away?" I went, and we prayed, and the Lord gave great comfort and courage in that hour.

The fourth day had passed. Late in the night the telephone rang again. When I lifted the receiver, a voice at the telephone office said, "Hold the line for long distance." When connection was made, a friend five hundred miles away said: "Mother is to undergo a very serious operation early in the morning. We are calling to ask you to pray for the surgeon, the nurses, mother, and the members of the family. We want God's will to be done. That's all. Good night."

I went back to my room that night, fell to my knees at the side of the bed and said: "Lord, teach me to pray. I had rather know how to pray than to know how to preach, for I can pray at any hour, day or night, and, at best, I can preach only a few hours each day."

"Lord, teach us to pray" (Luke 11:1). "Prayer was made without ceasing of the church unto God for him" (Acts 12:5).

"PRAY FOR YOURSELF!"

Some years ago I was conducting a revival in a church that had a feeling that the Lord visited that community to save people only one week in the summer of each year. The season for the revival in this particular community for years had been the week following the fourth Sunday in July. So we began the meeting, according to custom, on that date.

The meeting was making good progress, and the Lord was there in great power. He was saving the people. Great rejoicing was in the hearts of many.

One evening, a wicked young man and the leader of the wild crowd of the community, came to the service, and the Lord placed his hand upon him. The young man was poignantly convicted of sin. He felt the fearful remorse of a sinner. He knew that he was lost and that something had to be done at once.

In this plight, the young man arose from his pew in the rear of the small church and went down the aisle with fear and trembling. He took hold of the hand of the pastor and told him that he was lost and wanted everybody to pray for him. The minister called the congregation to prayer, and requested that all pray earnestly for the salvation of the convicted young man.

The ministers and the members of the congregation prayed, but there seemed to be no relief for the soul. Soon he called for his mother, who was a good Christian and a member of the church. She came immediately and prayed for him and began to talk to him about the Christ who could save him from sin.

The boy was not yet satisfied, and called for his father. The father was also a member of the church and a good Christian man. He gladly came to the aid of the lost boy.

A Christian sister was in the congregation, and she came to say a word about the love of Jesus and his desire to save the lost soul that would trust him. But the boy could feel no relief from the heavy burden of sin.

Soon the young man lifted his head and said, "Where is my brother?" Now his brother was a Christian young man, only a few years older than the lost boy. He was a matter-of-fact kind of fellow. But he was glad to come to the rescue of the lost soul.

When the brother came to the altar of the church, he looked into the face of the lost lad and said, "Bill, what is the matter with you?"

The brother answered, "I'm lost and condemned to hell."

The big brother said, "Well, what can I do about it?"

The answer came immediately, "It looks like you might pray for your own brother in such trouble!"

The big brother then took the convicted lad by the shoulders and shoved him to his knees, and said, "Pray for yourself!"

The young brother, with renewed hope, answered, "Well, I had not thought of that." He began to pray with great earnestness. He confessed his sin, wrong, and wickedness to the Lord. We then prayed the Lord to forgive his sin and save his soul. Needless to say, when the boy began thus to pour out his soul to Christ, his sin was taken away, and joy came into his soul. The angels of the Lord rejoiced over the one that was lost but was now found.

"I will pray with the spirit, and I will pray with the understanding" (1 Cor. 14:15).

"Praying always with all prayer and supplication in the Spirit" (Eph. 6:18).

PRAYING MEN

There is a most unusual and interesting crew of men who labor on the streets of Louisville. The crew is made up of both white and black men. We are informed by reliable persons that this group of men comes to the place of their work for the day early in the morning, several minutes before time to go to work, gathers in a band on the street, and spends the time in prayer. The men stand with uncovered heads, and several lead in prayer. Then someone of the group will make a brief talk. When the time comes to go to work, the men go from prayer to the labor of the day.

We do not know about the homelife of these men. We cannot tell whether they gather the family about a sacred altar and pray before they go out for the labor of the day. We do not know how devoted they are to the church of Christ on Sunday. We do not know how they support the cause of Christ with their labor. There are many things we do not know about them personally, but of this we are sure—theirs is a fine way to begin the labor of the day.

It would be hard for a man to go from a place of prayer to curse and fret and piddle on the job all day. Surely a man who prays about his work before he goes to the task will desire to do an honest day's work and give the very best there is in him. If all men would begin the task of the day with prayer, our nation would have a gracious citizenship, and the kingdom of God would go forward with leaps and bounds.

"Men ought always to pray, and not to faint" (Luke 18:1). "Pray one for another" (James 5:16). "I will therefore that men pray every where, lifting up holy hands, without wrath and doubting" (1 Tim. 2:8).

THE LORD ANSWERED

Without knowledge of the real condition, I accepted the pastorate of a church in a city where affairs were anything but right and pleasant. The people had quit church attendance, ceased to support the church, left bills unpaid, and allowed the property to go without repair.

At the first meeting of the deacons after my going on the

field, an unspeakable total of bills long passed due were placed on the table. In a spirit of defeat, the deacons tried to suggest some way out. Finally one of them realized that the pastor was present, and said, "Pastor, what do you have to say?"

As quick as a flash, I replied: "The last dime of these bills must be paid, and paid quickly. The Lord cannot honor a dishonest church, and I will not serve as pastor of such church. You'll pay these bills and stand high in the esteem of the people of this community, or you will get another pastor!"

The next question was, "How shall we get the money to pay the bills?"

My answer was: "Trust the Lord, and tell the people. Send an itemized list of these bills to every member of the church and request them to bring the cash to the church and place it on the table next Sunday week."

One of the deacons said, "I don't think that will work, but I move we try it."

The facts were sent to the people, along with an appeal for each one to give freely to clear the church of damaging current debts. Other appeals were made personally from the pulpit and in other meetings. The night before the offering was to be made, I was discouraged about the outlook, and remained in the church on my face before the Lord until very late at night. Finally the Lord came to me, and said: "Go on home, boy, and get some rest. Those bills will be paid in three minutes tomorrow morning." And they were!

The Lord has promised his people, "It shall come to pass, that before they call, I will answer; and while they are yet speaking, I will hear" (Isa. 65:24).

THE MORNING WATCH

Every person who carries a watch will find it necessary occasionally to take it to a jeweler to be cleaned and regulated. This time came to me. An expert jeweler was sought, and when the watch was in perfect condition and ready to be delivered, the expert said, "When do you wind your watch?" I then told him it had been my custom to wind it every night before retiring. He assured me that most men have the same custom, and then hastened to advise me to wind the watch the first thing in the morning. He explained that the works of the watch would then act under stronger force of the spring during the rough handling of the day, and at night when it is placed aside, the weaker force of the spring would be sufficient. It was a new lesson to me in caring for a watch.

This same lesson may be well applied to our spiritual lives. We should be sure to fill well our minds and hearts with the strength of the Lord in the early morning so that we may have the most possible spiritual force during the trials and cares and labors of the day. Then at night when we are ready to sleep, we have only to thank the Lord for his marvelous strength given to us during the hours of the day, and to leave ourselves in his mercy for the hours of rest. However much we may pray at noontime and in the evening, we should be very certain to have moments of real joy with the Lord in prayer, fellowship, and communion at the beginning of the day.

"My voice shalt thou hear in the morning, O Lord; in the morning will I direct my prayer unto thee, and will look up" (Psalm 5:3).

14

Service

"HE SHOWED ME HIS HANDS"

It was in the summer of 1906, when I was engaged in teaching a summer term of a small public school in our county. Thoughts of the future were often given serious moments. The immediate future was of most concern. I had heard of a vacancy in a near-by village for the place of principal of a three-teacher school, and I determined to make an effort to secure the position for another year.

On a Saturday morning a new buggy and a good horse were secured, and I drove to the village to apply for the position as principal of the public school. The trustees were called together, and the application was made in person. The officials assured me that my application would receive first consideration. When the meeting was over, one of the trustees invited me to attend the revival services which were in progress at the Baptist church in the village. It was my pleasure to do so.

The congregation in the village was not large but very cordial and happy in the series of meetings. The singing was unusually good; all testimonies were hearty; the sermon was powerful; the spirit of true worship permeated the place. The trend of thought throughout the service was that of consecration of life to the Master. At the close of the sermon, the pastor called on me to lead in prayer that someone in the congregation at that time would yield himself to the Lord for Christian service. The prayer was the most earnest I knew how to pray, for we were in the spirit of the hour. Soon the service came to a close, and all went away to their homes.

Thus, in the beaming sun of the eleventh hour of that hot summer day, I left to drive alone back to that quiet country place. And Jesus came and sat by my side. He seemed so real to me. He talked with me along the way. All other things were forgotten, and my thoughts were on him. It was a glorious drive with a wonderful Companion. He showed me his hands that were nailed to the cross. He said, "This suffering was all for the sake of the sinning men of the world." He then called me to go and make known this fact to lost sinners. I wept at the thought of the Saviour of the world asking me to have a part in his glorious work.

In the face of this glorious experience, it was in my heart to ask to be excused, not because I did not want a part in the great work, but because I felt so unworthy and unfit for the sublime task. The excuse was made, "I am only a poor country boy with insufficient education and no funds with which to go to school." It was further argued, "I am too timid ever to speak to a large congregation." When all excuses were given, the Master said, "Go and do the best you can, and leave the result with me."

The experience was over. The Master had called. The journey was ended. I had made a definite decision to enter the glorious ministry of the Lord Jesus Christ. I requested the trustees of the school to drop my name, and I entered a Baptist school to prepare for my life work.

"And God hath set some in the church, first apostles, secondarily prophets, thirdly teachers, after that miracles, then gifts of healings, helps, governments, diversities of tongues" (1 Cor. 12:28).

The words of that beautiful poem always come teeming into my mind in connection with this experience:

I had walked life's path with easy tread,
Had followed where comfort and pleasure led,
And then it chanced in a quiet place,
I met my Master face to face.

With station and rank and wealth for a goal,
Much thought for the body and none for the soul,
I had entered to win in life's mad race,
When I met my Saviour face to face.

I had built my castles and reared them high,
With their towers had pierced the blue of the sky,
I had sworn to rule with an iron mace,
When I met my Master face to face.

Met Him and knew him, and blushed to see
That eyes full of sorrow were fixed on me,
And I faltered and fell at his feet that day,
While all of my castles vanished away.

Melted and vanished, in their place
I saw naught else but my Master's face;
And I cried aloud, "Oh, make me meet
To follow the marks of Thy wounded feet."

My thought is now for the souls of men,
I have lost my life to find it again;
E'er since alone in a quiet place,
My Master and I stood face to face.

SAMUEL T. CARTER

HER BEST DOLL

Our little girl came home from kindergarten and said: "The teacher has requested dolls for the poor children, and I want to give one of mine. But I do not know which one to give."

All the dolls were placed before her and were admired lovingly. The best one was selected to be given. It was dressed with the nicest dress. She took it to dinner with her, cherished it by the fireside during the evening, and then took it to bed with her and held it close in sleep.

The next morning, before time to go to school, she held the doll close to her and wept, saying, "I am having a hard time parting with my best doll." I said to her, "You do not have to give your best doll." She replied, "But, Daddy, I would not want to give a sorry doll to any child."

The tears were dried, and in joy she skipped off to school to give her best doll for the poor children. She won the victory, and was very happy in the decision. When Christmas came, one of the best new dolls in all the city came to her as a gift of friends. When she saw it, she said, "I guess when you give your best, the best will come back to you."

That is the way it works. When we give our best for Christ, the best will come back to us. This is in accord with the words of Jesus, "Give, and it shall be given unto you" (Luke 6:38).

"I HAD RATHER WORK"

Some years ago we moved into a beautiful new residential section of Louisville, Kentucky. It was so new that the city had not had time to put in the sewerage system.

On the afternoon of July 2, a large truck stopped in front of our home, unloaded all the equipment, and soon twenty husky Negroes were digging away at a large ditch for the sewer. July the Fourth came, and all work ceased for the holiday. "Old Ben" was sent on the job to watch for the day. He came on at six o'clock in the morning. He first sat for a while, then arose, and walked up and down and took a look at the entire job. Soon he gathered his pick and shovel and went to work, alone.

At three o'clock in the afternoon I went out to talk with him. I assumed that he was sent on the job for the day to watch rather than to work, and made a remark to that effect. He replied: "Yes, sir, I get the same for watching that I do for working, but I get so tired sitting around, and I had rather work. We have better picks than this, but they are locked up, and I just use this one. I had rather use a sorry pick and work than to sit around all day and do nothing." Yes, he loved his work. If he loved the work of digging rock with a pick, surely Christian people should love the work of serving the Lord.

> God worketh; let me work too.
> God doeth; let me do.
> Busy for God my work I ply
> Till I rest in the rest of eternity.

"I must work the works of him that sent me, while it is day: the night cometh, when no man can work" (John 9:4).

MEN ARE HERE TO SERVE

It was my pleasure some days ago, on a train, to fall into company with a railroad official. He was in a good humor and wanted to talk, so it was mine to listen and learn. I soon found out that he began his service with the railroad as a water boy on a section. He has been promoted until now he is in charge of one department of the work of the road. More than six hundred men are under his direction.

His conversation was about his work, and he was full of his subject. He is a man of energy and ideals, and has no patience with a lazy useless fellow. He gave several examples of how he had to deal with men who were too sorry to do the task well. In some cases he had made men of them, and others he had to let go. He made this fine statement that has remained with me: "Men are here to serve."

The official then applied his statement and said, "It is true with the railroad from the lowest man to the highest official." He then stated that Masonry stands for service—to one another, to widows, to orphans, to the poor. "I do not know much about Christianity," he said, "but my idea is that the spirit of it is that of of service."

This is the ideal of Jesus. Men are here to serve the Lord Jesus Christ. "If any man desire to be first, the same shall be last of all, and servant of all" (Mark 9:35).

RESTING EASY

During my brief years in the service of the church of our Lord, it has ever been my desire to admonish all Baptists to live close to the Lord and his church. We have ever invited Baptists in our immediate community to bring their church membership to our church. Every excuse under the sun seems to have been offered for not doing this, but a new one was given to me sometime ago.

Information came to me that a woman at a given address was a Baptist, with her church membership out of the city. I called at the home and found that she had been there eight years. She had sold her farm and all else in the village and had moved everything to the city except her church membership. She even cared more for her dog than she did for her relation to the church of Christ, for she moved her dog, and cares for him daily.

It was also found that she had three grown sons in the home—lost, in the world without God, without Christ, and without hope. No effort was being made to bring them to Christ for salvation. When she was urged to bring her church membership to our church, which was near by, and to unite with the Lord's people and to seek to be useful for the Lord's kingdom, she very calmly gave the following excuse for not doing it: "My church membership is resting easy where it is."

Yes, her membership was resting; it certainly was not working. Not even her next-door neighbor knew that she was a church member. She seemed to be ashamed to let anyone know that she had loved Christ and his church.

Jesus said, "Whosoever therefore shall be ashamed of me and of my words in this adulterous and sinful generation; of him also shall the Son of man be ashamed, when he cometh in the glory of his Father with the holy angels" (Mark 8:38).

THAT RUINS THE SERMON

One Sunday morning I preached a sermon on spiritual gifts, and the service that morning was a high spiritual hour. The congregation was large, reverent, and worshipful. All the songs were appropriate, the special music was enjoyed by all, and the sermon was delivered with spiritual fervor.

When the service was over, a good deacon and his wife, who had been living together in the work of the Lord for more than fifty years, came to me at the door of the church. The deacon was most complimentary of the service of the morning, with special emphasis on the sermon.

After the deacon had completed his comments on the sermon, his wife chimed in and said: "Yes, it was a great sermon, but it makes me feel very small. I just wonder if I have found my spiritual gift, developed it, and used it for the glory of the Lord. I fear I have failed in the work of my Lord." The deacon then looked lovingly at his wife and said: "Why bring that up? That ruins the sermon. That makes all of us feel bad."

Many sermons are ruined when people fail to act on the high and holy impulse inspired in the most blessed moments of the worship hour in the church. The best way is to take the very best things of the worship hour into everyday life and to put them into action in daily life for the glory of God and the advancement of his kingdom.

"Now concerning spiritual gifts, brethren, I would not have you ignorant" (1 Cor. 12:1).

THE SERVANT OF ALL

In our community there was a very fine country home in which a good father and faithful mother had lived and served many years. Six children were given to the home, and each one of them had reached maturity. All were now away most of the time, either married, in school, or in some other activity, leaving the home with parents alone.

Hard by this country home was the home of their colored family. To this family eight children were given, and all were away out in the world except one son, who lived in the small house in the yard of the owner.

Just before Christmas it became known in the home that the Negro man expected to be married on Christmas Day and bring his bride to the house in the back yard. One of the fine Christian girls of the gracious country home was spending the holidays with her parents. She learned that the Negro man was going to bring his bride there.

The evening of Christmas Day found this unusual white Christian girl in the humble cottage of the Negro, sweeping, cleaning, placing fresh linen on the mantel, tables, bed, hanging pictures on the walls, and making the place home-like for the new colored housekeeper. Surely, the love of Christ and the Christian ideals for a Christian home inspired the young lady to the task.

"Whosoever of you will be the chiefest, shall be servant of all" (Mark 10:44). "Whosoever will be chief among you, let him be your servant" (Matt. 20:27).

WILLING TO DO IT

It was one Sunday morning in 1917 that a request came to me from the United States Government to go as a chaplain in the army with the boys to Europe during World War I. The request disturbed me, and I filed it and tried to forget it. But as I prayed the Lord to let me know his will in the matter and to give me grace to do it, I was convinced that he wanted me to go.

Some nights later, as my good Christian companion and I were praying, she said to me: "You are troubled about something, and you have not let me know what it is. Tell me now! Your troubles are mine." I then told her that an appeal had come to me from Washington to join the army as a chaplain and to go to Europe with the boys. She immediately said: "You cannot go. You are exempt for more than one reason." We then agreed to pray over the matter and to try to know the will of the Lord and to be willing to do it. A few nights later, she arose from prayer and said, "The Lord wants you to go, and I must be willing."

The members of the church were then informed about the call, and after earnest prayer for days, the church gave a leave of absence for the period of the war.

On the morning I was to leave, many people were at the railroad station to tell me good-by. One of the deacons, a close friend, shook hands with me and turned away without speaking. As he went away from the station, he said to a close friend of his, "I never expect to see that boy again." Just to cheer me up, the friend came and told me what was said. It certainly was encouraging! I sent word back to the deacon that the Lord was leading and that he would take care of me in every danger of the front line and bring me back. That was done. The Lord was trusted. He took care of me in the gravest dangers.

Jesus said, "Lo, I am with you alway, even unto the end of the world" (Matt. 28:20).

15

Sin

"BUT I DON'T WANT TO!"

Some years ago it was my pleasure to spend some days in a good Christian home with a grandmother and grandfather. The grandchildren would often come into the home. On one occasion the mother had gone out, leaving the very young son in care of grandmother for the afternoon. Like all boys, the fine youngster began to feel his keeping and sought to assert himself. But the good grandmother was equal to the occasion, and started for the rod. The boy immediately quieted down, and the grandmother said, "Are you going to be good?" He replied, "Yes, I will be good, but I don't want to!" Lots of human nature!

The apostle Paul experienced the two natures warring for supremacy in his life. He wrote about it. It is the battle of the ages. He said, "I delight in the law of God . . . : but I see another law in my members, warring against the law of my mind, and bringing me into captivity to the law of sin which is in my members" (Rom. 7:22-23).

But Paul found the way out of that dilemma and pointed it out for all others who will follow. "The law of the Spirit of life in Christ Jesus hath made me free from the law of sin and death" (Rom. 8:2). "There is therefore now no condemnation to them which are in Christ Jesus, who walk not after the flesh, but after the Spirit" (Rom. 8:1).

When Christ sets the soul free from the law of sin and death, the soul then does not desire to do the evil thing and to follow after the things of the flesh.

"DON'T LET ME DIE!"

During my days in college there were some churches in small towns in the central part of Alabama which were good enough to call me to preach for them on Sundays and to be their pastor in the summer. While spending the summer in one of these small towns, it was my pleasure to spend much time with the boys of the church and community.

Being a young man without experience and knowledge in the work of the ministry, I learned, to my utter surprise, that there were some boys who were afraid of the minister. For the life of me, I could never see why. In this particular village there was a young fellow of this type, about my age. He avoided me. He would turn away when he saw me coming. He never went to church or Sunday school. He defied the Bible and denied God. I learned that he was the devil's chief envoy in that community. Nothing was too wicked for him to do. The boy was employed at a small mill just out of town. One afternoon, while he was doing his regular work, a belt came off the pulley and struck him with great force on the left chest, lacerated the flesh, tore the muscles away, cut the main artery leading from the heart, threw him to the ground, and left him half conscious and fast bleeding to death. There were only two doctors in the small town, and neither of them could be found. No one knew how to stop the bleeding.

News of the fearful accident spread to every part of the community in a very few minutes. Many people went out to see, and to help if possible. His mother was there in a short time. Other members of the family were present. Everyone showed great anxiety for the boy.

When I arrived, the head of the boy was in the lap of his mother, and they were both covered with his blood. The mother was helpless. Her heart was breaking, while his was bleeding. She caressed the bloody brow of the boy while he begged with a pitiful and ever-weakening voice, "O Mother, don't let me die! Mother, please don't let me die!"

Death was inevitable. The gathered multitude could only stand by and look on. It was too late for anyone there to do any good for the dying boy. As we looked into his face, there came an inexpressibly horrible look on his face. He made a mighty surge, and cried aloud, saying, "Mother! Mother! I'm in hell!" With that scream, his hands fell, his breath left him, and he finished his course on earth. His soul took the last plunge into a terrible eternity.

Sad beyond expression was that event to the heart of the mother, and to all who looked on the scene. Even sadder than this is it when any soul has to face what the soul of that young man went into. It was all because of sin, denial of the Christ, refusing to accept the plan of God for the salvation of the soul. It will be even so with all who are in the world without God, without Christ, and without hope—and do not seek for salvation.

"The wages of sin is death" (Rom. 6:23). "Whatsoever a man soweth, that shall he also reap" (Gal. 6:7). This boy had sown to the flesh, and now he was beginning his long harvest of eternal punishment.

There is a way to escape the horrible death and consequent punishment of a sinner, and that is to accept the atoning work of Christ, for "while we were yet sinners, Christ died for us. Much more then, being now justified by his blood, we shall be saved from wrath through him" (Rom. 5:8-9).

GIVE THE DEVIL CREDIT

There are many experiences that come to one during college days that are never forgotten. Lifetime friendships are formed in college. These charming days are always remembered. It is about one thing that happened in college that I desire to speak. Among my many friends there I was much delighted with the friendship of one who had the delightful characteristic of never speaking evil about anyone. He could always find something good to say about every person. If he could not, he would not speak at all. That is a good rule of life.

One day we were going to the class in theology. That day the lesson happened to be about the devil. As we went along, I said to one of my friends, "Here is one place where friend _____ will not speak, for he never says anything bad about anyone, and he certainly cannot find anything good to say about the devil." We went on to the class, and the discussion went along in the usual way for sometime.

I could see my friend occasionally run his fingers through his hair as if he had something to say. A few minutes later, he was leaning forward and seeking to get in his word about the devil. I said to myself, "Here is where he is going to break the rule of his life." When he arose, he said, "Fellows, you'll have to give the devil credit for one thing!" With astonishment, I listened to hear a good word about the devil. For the Lord's sake, what will it be? He then continued, "You have to give him credit for being on his job all the time." The entire class admitted that the statement was true. The devil is on his job every hour of the day and every day of the year.

"Be sober, be vigilant; because your adversary the devil, as a roaring lion, walketh about, seeking whom he may devour" (1 Peter 5:8).

"I AM A LOST SINNER"

Some weeks ago one of the Christian workers in a hospital called me and told me that they had a lost, ruined, undone man in the hospital who was near death and requested me to come to see him.

When I arrived at the room in the hospital, I found a frail, wretched, weak, and worn frame of a man. Conditions in the room revealed that he was suffering from an unspeakable disease, and the expression of his countenance revealed that his soul was in the throes of a disease more horrible than that of his body. When asked how he was getting along, he began to tell how he was getting along physically.

When he had completed this story, I asked, "How is it with your soul?" He answered amid bitter sobs: "Minister, I am a lost sinner. I am sick unto death, and will die and go into the presence of the good Lord unprepared. I have had a chance to live the right kind of life, but I have wasted every opportunity that ever came my way. I guess it would have been far better had I never lived. I have ruined my own life and, along with it, the lives of others." He broke down and cried, and wept and wailed most bitterly.

I then asked him if he could trust the Saviour and let him save his soul. I told him of the thief on the cross and how he trusted Jesus to save him, even in the last hour of his life. I told him of the love, willingness, and anxiety of the Saviour to save him. He wept bitterly again, and said, "The good Lord might save my soul if I had strength to get hold of him, but my life is wasted and gone forever."

"For whatsoever a man soweth, that shall he also reap" (Gal. 6:7).

"I'VE WAITED TOO LATE"

Some years ago I was conducting a revival meeting in a country community. The entire population was attending the services. It was at a time of the year when the people were not busy about their farm work. Prayer meetings were conducted in the homes during the afternoons. In this way many people were reached that could never have been reached by the services in the church.

One afternoon we were in a home in the community, and the service was held with the people on the back porch, which was shaped like an L. Some songs had been sung and many of the people had given testimonies and led in prayer. After this, I got out on the ground before all the people and began the sermon of the afternoon.

As I was talking, a very old man came up behind me in the yard and sat on a stump that was near. About the close of my talk, he touched me on the arm with his cane and asked if he might speak. I had never seen him before and did not know him, but I assured him that he might speak. By some effort, he arose, and leaning on the stump, he pointed his cane toward the people on the porch and said words like these: "Young people, let me ask you to do what this young man is asking you to do and accept Christ as your Saviour now while you can. I saw the day back yonder when I could have been saved, but I've waited too late, and now I am doomed to ruin. There is nothing but eternal perdition for me." With these words he was overcome, and came near falling, but we assisted him to be seated.

Many times during the week I talked with the old man personally and sought to get him to pray and accept Christ, but every time he would give the same answer: "I've waited too late. I'll never be saved. There's nothing but ruin for me." So far as I have been able to learn, the man left this life in that condition.

"Seek ye the Lord while he may be found, call ye upon him while he is near" (Isa. 55:6).

NO TIME FOR JESUS

Twenty years ago a young man came from the country to our city. Later, his parents and the other members of the family came. This young man cared for his parents, brothers, sisters, and friends; but he gave no thought to Christ or the welfare of his soul or the work of the church.

One morning he went to his work at eight o'clock. A few minutes later he felt sick and went to his car to rest until he should feel better. But he grew worse instead of better and so decided to go home. At noon the doctor was called to his bedside. The doctor could do nothing for him, and he passed away at three o'clock that afternoon, without God, without Christ, and without hope.

When I arrived at the home, the feeble father was trying to find something good to say about the forty-four-year-old son who had neglected the most important thing in all life. The weeping father said: "He was good to his mother and to me. He was liberal, for I heard him say that he put a dollar on the collection plate when he was at church the last time five years ago. He was a member of the Masonic Order and had lots of friends there. He has always been a good hearted boy." All I could ask was, "What did he do with Christ? Did he profess faith in Christ and accept him for personal salvation?" The answer was negative.

Forty-four years on this earth, and not one day in which to face the Christ who died to save his soul from sin! No time or thought for the Christ and his church! "He that believeth on the Son hath everlasting life: and he that believeth not the Son shall not see life; but the wrath of God abideth on him" (John 3:36).

16

Stewardship

A NICKEL TO PUT IN

It was my pleasure some Sundays ago to attend a Sunday school class of men. On that particular Sunday, since I was to speak to the class, the large class of women in the church was invited to meet with the men. In the church membership and in the class is a man who is very wealthy, possibly more than a millionaire. He has never been known to get any real joy from the giving of his money to the great and good causes of this life. His joy seems to come in hoarding his riches.

On this Sunday I sat near this man and his wife in the class. As he made his report, and began to search his purse for an offering, he could not find a nickel, and I heard him say to his wife: "I cannot find a nickel to put in. Have you one?" She assured him that she had provided the correct change, and immediately produced it.

Two days later we were guests of this good brother at luncheon, and we just happened to learn that not less than fifteen dollars were spent for the meal. Fifteen dollars for one meal, and five cents for the church!

Not for one moment would I permit the reader to think I do not appreciate the kindness and hospitality of this good friend, nor would I cast reflection on his act. But, as I told him, I am using this to show how ready we are to lavish riches on ourselves and the things we love and to let the cause of Christ go begging. This seems to be the spirit of America now.

A TITHER BECOMES A CHRISTIAN

When you read this title, you feel that it is not stated correctly. You would think it should read "A Christian Becomes a Tither." But the former is just what happened in our church some years ago.

In the offerings of the church the treasurer had been finding, as often as once a month for several months, a roll of bills totaling as much as twenty-five or thirty dollars. The deacons were alerted to watch very carefully to see if they could learn who was placing the money on the collection plate. Sure enough, in less than a month, the roll was dropped on the plate again, but the keen eye of a deacon saw the person place it there.

The offering was made by a man. He was pointed out to me, and later when I talked with him, I found that he was not a Christian but felt that at least one dollar out of every ten he earned belonged to the Lord and should be given to the church. Thus, he was honest with the Lord and religiously tithed his salary each month. When the way of the Lord in salvation was made plain to him, he immediately accepted Christ as personal Saviour. He joined the church and became active in Christian service.

It is a rebuke to Christians that even unsaved people feel that they must give at least one tenth of their income to the Lord. This should inspire every Christian to honor God with his substance. "Blessed are all they that put their trust in him" (Psalm 2:12).

ABOUNDING IN THE GRACE OF GIVING

A good Christian woman who was a devoted and loyal member of our church had not been able to attend the worship services of the church for several weeks. As soon as she was able to be out, she made her way to the church, went into the office of the secretary, and said: "I desire to pay my church dues for the past few weeks. I am too far behind."

Then, as she began to count the money to turn over to the Lord's treasury, she said, "I do not get so far behind with my personal bills, for I pay for rent, gas, water, light, groceries, milk, and butter as soon as the bills are due. I know the Lord's money should be brought to the Lord's house on the Lord's Day, but since I have not been able to come, I have placed it aside and kept it until I could get here with it."

This good woman is a widow, living in modest rented rooms, and working with her own hands for the most of her income. But she abounds in faith, and knowledge, and in all diligence, and in love; thus she abounds in this grace of giving also.

"See that ye abound in this grace also" (2 Cor. 8:7).

AN ASSEMBLAGE OF POOR THINGS

Some years ago it was my pleasure to lead a country church in a small building program for adding some Sunday school rooms. It was a very small undertaking for the church, for the members were well able to do far more. The members of the church had money to give to the building fund, but they did not want to turn it loose. For this reason, some objected to the advance step, and others tried to avoid it. It has been true since Mary anointed the feet of Jesus that always someone will object to any good thing that is to be done.

Someone made a suggestion that the members of the church be allowed to give such things as they had on the farm, and that these articles be sent to market and sold for money to be used in the building. There was no objection to this, especially for those who could do no better. A special day was set apart and a place appointed to take charge of the goods and make the sale. Each person was to bring his offering to the central place.

The day came for the people to bring the Lord's goods together, and it was a most glorious morning. There was every evidence of the great love of a great Father. The sun was bright; the morning air was fresh; nature was doing her best to show that every good and every perfect gift is from above and cometh from God.

Many members of the church gathered at the central place early in the morning to see what would happen. Soon the things began to arrive from every part of the community. They came from east, west, north, and south. Some on foot, some in cars, some in wagons, some in buggies— the gifts came every way.

Surely no one on earth has ever seen before or since such an assemblage of poor things that were to be given to the Lord. Poor pigs, old hens, aged roosters, nubbin corn, small potatoes, sorry hay, and a shabby lot of other things were assembled. One old rooster actually died on the way.

When the things were all in and ready for the committee

to start to market, the entire affair had the appearance of the ragged end of destruction. My face was filled with shame. I wanted to deny the whole crowd. I was sorry that the people who called themselves Christians were not willing to give the cause of Christ the very best they had. Should it be so? Is Christ not worthy of our best?

Even in olden days, the people would not offer as a sacrifice to the Lord a lamb with even a blemish. The command about the burnt sacrifice was, "Let him offer a male without blemish." The meal offering was to be of "fine flour." The very best was to be presented before the Lord. The sacrifice had to be perfect. Now, in this day of his marvelous grace, surely he is more than worthy of our very best. We should give him the best hour of the day, the best years of our lives, the best boy of the family, the best girl of the home—even the very best we have of everything, for he is worthy.

"I beseech you therefore, brethren, by the mercies of God, that ye present your bodies a living sacrifice, holy, acceptable unto God, which is your reasonable service" (Rom. 12:1).

"I LOVE YOU SO MUCH"

Many years ago, Mrs. Williams and I conducted a revival in a small village in east Kentucky. Regular services were conducted at the church at ten o'clock in the morning, three in the afternoon, and seven in the evening. A great revival was evident, and we were using every means possible to reach the lost.

One of the most far-reaching services was the one conducted for the children in the afternoon. The children of

the church and community assembled and listened atten-
tively to the simple story of Christ and his power and
desire to save. We taught them to sing songs and to pray
the simple prayer with a child's faith.

Thus, seeking to become all things to all men that we
might win some, the Lord blessed the services and gave a
gracious revival. Many souls were won to Christ and to
the church. Lives were consecrated to the service of the
Master. Homes were made better. The entire community
enjoyed a spiritual uplift.

At the closing service of the revival, an opportunity was
given for the people to express their appreciation with a gift
to the helpers. The offering was ample, for the men,
women, and children of every denomination of the community were generous. Our hearts were made glad with
the kindness and generosity of the people.

The closing service was conducted at the eleven o'clock
hour, and we were to leave for home in the afternoon. A
great crowd gathered at the station to tell us good-by. One
among the first to come to the station where we were
waiting was a little, frail, poorly clad, embarrassed girl.
She took her stand near Mrs. Williams and would not
leave. Often she would look up into her face as if she
wanted to say something.

As the train was nearing the station, Mrs. Williams put
her arm about the little girl and said, "Dear, do you want
to say something to me?"

The little one threw her arms about her, looked into her
face most earnestly, and said, "Yes'm, I wish I had something to give you."

Mrs. Williams replied, "You can just give me the love of
your precious heart, and that will make me happy!"

The little girl replied: "I do love you. I love you more than anyone now, since my mother is gone."

But the little one wanted to give some material thing. She sought a way to express the sincere love of her heart. She then held her left hand up toward the face of Mrs. Williams and, with the fingers of the right hand, took hold of a valueless ring on her pale finger. Looking at it, she said: "This is the best thing I have. Mother gave it to me, and I love it. But I love you so much that I want you to have it.

This is the way love behaves. It would be a great day for the kingdom of God if the followers of Christ would come to him with all they have and say: "Lord here is my life. It is the best thing I have. I love it, but I love thee so much more that I want you to have it. Accept my all, O Christ!"

Christ demands that his followers put him and his cause before all else. Jesus said, "If any man come to me, and hate not his father, and mother, and wife, and children, and brethren, and sisters, yea, and his own life also, he cannot be my disciple" (Luke 14:26). He also said, "If a man love me, he will keep my words" (John 14:23).

THE BIBLE WAY

The Bible is very clear in teaching the time, the way, and the amount of money individual Christians should give into the treasury of the Lord. It is just as clear as it is in the teaching of baptism, salvation, heaven, and other subjects. We Baptists do not contend for the Bible way of giving as earnestly as we do for the Bible way of baptism.

It was my pleasure the other day to look into the treasurer's book of one of the great Baptist churches of our city. The record of one giver was pointed out. The giver is a successful lawyer. We observed the record of his weekly offering to the church for many weeks. The smallest weekly offering on his record, that we saw, was $68, and the largest was $276. We were told that the good man makes it a practice on every Saturday afternoon, the last thing before leaving his office, to look at his bank book, total the entire deposits for that week, and write a check for one tenth of that amount to take to his church in his offering envelope on Sunday morning. He gives one tenth of his gross income into the treasury of the Lord.

We most highly commend the example of this good man. He is a regular, systematic, liberal, and proportionate giver to the treasury of the Lord. He worships the Lord with his money, which represents his time, talent, energy, love, and devotion. He first gave himself to the Lord, and then he gives continually to the Lord, who makes it possible for him to live, work, and serve.

"Upon the first day of the week let every one of you lay by him in store, as God hath prospered him" (1 Cor. 16:2).

"WE DON'T HAVE TO PAY PREACHERS"

When I was a student in college, my home association invited me to preach the introductory sermon at the annual meeting. The meeting was conducted that year in a church about seven miles from our home.

I felt very important to leave college on a mission like this. The day was fine. Someone met me at the railroad station early in the morning, and we went out to where the association was in session. I met there my father, two brothers, and one sister.

The association was organized with a great crowd present. Letters were presented, visitors were recognized, and the time for the sermon came. The Lord gave me a message, and liberty in delivering it. When the sermon was over, the moderator called for a collection to pay expenses of the boy from college, and the treasurer gave me $5.86.

The fellowship of the meeting was delightful. During the dinner hour, one man, who did not want his right hand to know what his left did, gave me a nickel, and said, "The Lord bless you, young man." A good sister called me to one side and told me that she did not have any money at that time, but that she would have when she sold cotton, and she would not forget me then. But I guess she did. Others made similar promises.

The day soon went by, the afternoon session was over, and we were on our way home in the old family hack. One of my younger brothers, riding on the rear seat of the shay, said with an air of distinction and pride: "We don't have to pay preachers. We have them in our family!" But, upon investigation, it was found that the members of my own family had given $2.75 of the total.

That is the way things go. The one who is most interested will do more. The one who loves most will give most. The cause of Christ is supported today by those who love him most. It is easy to give of our best to the cause we love dearest.

"And he answering said, Thou shalt love the Lord thy

God with all thy heart, and with all thy soul, and with all thy strength, and with all they mind; and thy neighbour as thyself" (Luke 10:27).

WHAT WE CAN GIVE FOR JESUS

One of the Sunday school teachers in our church gave this question to the members of a class of Primary children: What can you give to Jesus?

A bright little fellow wrote the following:

> I can give my heart to Jesus.
> I can give my thoughts to Jesus.
> I can give my words to Jesus.
> I can give my deeds to Jesus.
> I can give my money to Jesus.

Could you write a better statement than this Primary wrote? Heart, thought, words, deeds, money! What more could Jesus ask? What joy his heart would experience should all give these! But he demands all. He will be first. We must put him first in life, before all else and everyone else, if we are to be pleasing disciples to him.

Also, this note of the child shows that many children of our day use the privileges and opportunities of this age to a good advantage. With homes, schools, churches, Sunday schools, Training Unions, choirs, and mission classes, every child in the land should be given a chance to meet Jesus and fall in love with him.

Jesus said, "Suffer little children, and forbid them not, to come unto me: for of such is the kingdom of heaven" (Matt. 19:14).